TEACH THEM TO BE HAPPY

by

Robert A. Sullo

New View Publications
Chapel Hill, North Carolina

This book is for Laurie

Illustrations by Laurie A. Sullo

Typography by Desktop Publishing, Inc., Carrboro, NC.

Library of Congress Cataloging-in-Publication Data
Sullo, Robert A., 1951-
    Teach them to be happy
    1. Happiness in children 2. Child rearing
I. Title.
BF723.H37S85 1989   649'.123   89-61056
ISBN 0-944337-04-X

Author Speaking Engagements
For information regarding speaking engagements by Robert A. Sullo, contact the author at P.O. Box 1336, Sandwich, MA 02563 or phone (508) 888-7627.

Quantity Purchases
Special terms are available when ordering quantities of this title. For information contact the Sales Department, New View Publications, P.O. Box 3021, Chapel Hill, N.C. 27515-3021.

Manufactured in the United States of America.

Acknowledgments

Dr. William Glasser's speaking and writing about Reality Therapy and Control Theory have helped me become a better parent and happier person. I want to express my sincere thanks to Dr. Glasser for sharing his insights in an articulate, concise and helpful way.

The following people have been especially important to me in my growing understanding of Control Theory and Reality Therapy: Nancy Buck, David Hardy, Al Katz, and David Moran. Thanks to all of you.

Valuable input was provided along the way by:

Sandy Boucher, Director, Sandy's School, Wareham, MA

Flo Szabo, Early Childhood Specialist, Plymouth Public Schools, Plymouth, MA

Shirley Keifer, Dallas Center-Grimes Kindergarten, Iowa

Valerie Fairhurst of Antioch Corporation, Cataumet, MA, deserves a special note of thanks for hours of help, feedback, criticism, and the contribution of developmentally appropriate activities.

This never would have been possible without the support, encouragement, and enthusiasm of Perry and Fred Good. Thanks also to Nancy Salmon, whose intelligent editing made this book more readable, more accurate and shorter! Thanks for believing in the value of this project.

I'm fortunate to have parents who have given me the encouragement and support every child should receive. Thank you for teaching me to be happy.

Finally, Laurie, Kristy, Greg, and Melanie have helped more than they know. I am thankful for having such a needs-satisfying family.

Forward

Knowing how to be happy is not as mysterious as it appears to be. In *Teach Them to Be Happy*, Bob Sullo gives teachers and parents of young children a simple guide for systematically teaching children what they need and what they can do to be happy.

After writing *In Pursuit of Happiness*, I met Bob Sullo who is a school psychologist with fifteen years experience in public education. I asked him if he would write a companion book based on my book with examples and activities that would be applicable to young children. He was enthusiastic. *Teach Them To Be Happy* is the result.

I hope that using these ideas with your own children or those you teach will be as exciting, gratifying and fun for you as it has been for us.

Perry Good
Chapel Hill, NC

June 1989

"It is not easy to find happiness in ourselves and it is not possible to find it elsewhere."

Agnes Repplier
The Treasure Chest

Table Of Contents

Part I: Using Control Theory and Reality Therapy
With Young Children 1

Part II: Teach Them To Be Happy

Introduction: Our Basic Needs 15

Chapter One: Signals 33

Chapter Two: Pictures 48

Chapter Three: Behavior 62

Chapter Four: Balance 74

Chapter Five: Options 87

Chapter Six: Relationships 100

Chapter Seven: Creativity 115

Activities for a Balanced Classroom 120

PART I

USING CONTROL THEORY
AND REALITY THERAPY WITH
YOUNG CHILDREN

Young children, and even many adults, frequently believe that happiness is something that just "happens" to them, that it is unrelated to what they are doing. For all of us, however, happiness is achieved by satisfying our needs in a responsible way. Even young children can learn how to behave responsibly and can gain more effective control in their lives when they make the connection between how they choose to behave and the level of happiness they experience.

I have written this book for professional educators, parents and other adults who care deeply about and spend time with children three years old through grade three. This is a book about teaching young children how to be happy. After reading and using this book, you will find that the children you deal with will begin to act more responsibly, will begin to understand the basic needs which motivate them, and will begin to see that they are very much in control of the behaviors they choose and the happiness they will experience the rest of their lives.

The ideas in this book are based largely on Dr. William Glasser's work in Reality Therapy and Control Theory. More specifically, this book builds upon E. Perry Good's *In Pursuit of Happiness*. A lively, animated, and exciting book, *In Pursuit of Happiness* has become a favorite of mine. My goal with *Teach Them To Be Happy* has been to write a book for parents and early childhood educators that will be as valuable to use with children as *In Pursuit of Happiness* is with teens and adults. Read *In Pursuit of Happiness* before you attempt to teach these concepts to your children. It will give you an introduction to Control Theory so that you will be more comfortable with it before beginning to use it. *In Pursuit of Happiness* contains a variety of exercises for adults, giving you an opportunity to put the theory into practice. You will then experience what you will ask your children to do, so you will better understand their joys and struggles.

As an educator for the past fifteen years and a parent of three children, two of them preschoolers, I feel strongly about the ideas presented in the following pages. The most telling comment I can make is that I use these ideas in my own life, with my own children, and I am a happier person and a better parent as a result. I sincerely hope that I can find the words to make these concepts come alive for you as well. If I am successful, your lives and the lives of the children you touch will be happier—and that's what this book is all about!

Control Theory and Reality Therapy

In order to help you understand how teaching Control Theory and Reality Therapy concepts to young children fosters their cognitive development and leads to greater happiness for both you and the children, I want to begin with a general overview so that you will have a frame of reference. In Part II, I will explain various aspects of Control Theory in more detail.

Control Theory contends that all of our behavior is internally motivated. We are all born with certain needs, both physical and psychological, which must be satisfied. All of our behavior can be understood as our best attempt, at any given moment, to meet our needs. Although most people recognize and acknowledge their physical needs (hunger, thirst, sleep, warmth, sex), they may not realize they have basic psychological needs which also must be satisfied. The four basic psychological needs are: love or belonging, power or competence, freedom, and fun. While not all behavior is effective or responsible, it always represents an individual's attempt to satisfy one or more basic needs. Even "crazy" behavior offers some people what seems at the time to be their best opportunity to meet their basic psychological needs. Control Theory teaches us that when people have better, more effective, more responsible behaviors available to them to satisfy their needs, they will give up the less responsible, less effective behaviors. Our role, then, is to help people, even very young ones, develop better behavioral choices as they try continuously to satisfy their basic needs.

Reality Therapy is the application of the principles of

3

Control Theory. It is a process which includes asking people to examine what it is that they want, what behaviors they are currently using to get what they want, then evaluating the effectiveness of their current behaviors. Once a person, young or old, realizes and admits that their current behaviors are not the most effective, responsible behaviors available, we can help them choose more effective behaviors and make better plans so they can get more of what they want.

It is frequently difficult to get people to give up their current behavioral choices, even ineffective ones. Remember, they are using those behaviors because they seem to offer them the best chance of satisfying their needs. It takes a lot of hard work and commitment to get people to risk new behaviors. The good news is that you can teach an old dog new tricks. Even adults will make major changes in how they choose to live their lives once they become convinced that there is a better way and that they will have friendship and support along the way. Young children, who are less likely to be stuck in ineffective behavioral patterns than are adults, will learn quickly to make more responsible choices if given good instruction. Even very young children can learn the basics of Control Theory and start to understand that their happiness is a direct product of what they choose to do. Armed with that powerful knowledge, young children are less likely to blame others when things go wrong. They are less likely to wait passively for things to improve. They are more likely to take effective action, choosing responsible behaviors that lead to happiness.

Control theory is very different from stimulus-response theory, currently the most widely practiced and advocated psychological approach in America. Most educators have had some training in stimulus-response theory and many practice this approach routinely. Parents, too, are often attracted by this apparently "common sense" approach to understanding what motivates human behavior. Briefly, stimulus-response theory asserts that when we reward behaviors they will increase in frequency. Conversely, we use punishment to decrease the frequency of behaviors. Essentially, stimulus-response theory

4

contends that we are controlled by outside forces, shaped by the systematic (or accidental) presentation of rewards and punishments.

Control Theory teaches that we are internally, not externally motivated. Whereas stimulus-response theory suggests that we are reactive creatures, looking to gain rewards from others or avoid their punishment, according to Control Theory we choose our behavior because we believe it will help us satisfy our basic needs. Stimulus-response theory claims that we react; Control Theory teaches us that all we can do is act.

Let's examine for a moment what happens to children who have been raised by parents who employ a stimulus-response approach to child rearing and have been educated by teachers who favor the same approach. How do these children behave once they reach adolescence? More often than not they become rebellious, frequently defiant, and certainly less manageable. Following a stimulus-response approach, many parents and educators try to devise more effective punishers only to meet increased resistance. Why? If we can just give up the notion that people are externally controlled and accept that we are all internally motivated, the answer is not particularly mysterious. All of us satisfy our needs by behaving, sometimes alone, but frequently with others. When we punish adolescents, we automatically frustrate their needs for love, fun, freedom, and power, and they will choose to defy us, having faith that their needs can be satisfied elsewhere, particularly in their peer group, a social network much larger than what was available to them as young children. Children in preschool and in the primary grades also choose, but because they frequently choose what we want, we mistakenly believe that we control them. In reality, young children often behave the way we want them to because they rely upon us to help them satisfy their needs, an aspect of their world which will change in time. If stimulus-response theory were valid, it would be valid throughout a person's life. Experience shows us, however, that people do what they want to do, not what we want them to do. Even when they do what we want, they don't do it because we want them

5

to. They do it because they believe it is the most satisfying behavior they have available at the time.

You may find yourself at this point asking the following question: "If punishment is ineffective and children are going to do what they want anyway, should we accept irresponsible, disruptive behavior and sit back idly while children make poor behavioral choices?" The answer is, "Absolutely not!" Discipline is both effective and essential. Unlike punishment, discipline works because it involves natural consequences (all behaviors have consequences) and it teaches responsibility.

"In nature there are neither rewards nor
punishments — there are consequences."
— Robert G. Ingersoll

An example may help clarify the difference between punishment and discipline and their respective effectiveness. "Time-out" is a punishment frequently used with young children. Essentially, the misbehaving child is cut off from all activities and reinforcers for a prescribed period of time. Once the "sentence" has been served, the child rejoins the group, no wiser, a bit more angry, with his self-esteem just a bit more compromised.

A frequently used Control Theory alternative to time-out is a planning center. Here, the misbehaving child is removed from the group but is not punished in any way. In the planning center the misbehaving child must come up with a plan for acceptable behavior in order to rejoin the group. Of course, most young children will need help developing a plan. In the planning center an involved, caring adult helps children learn more responsible ways to satisfy their needs. There is no attempt to punish, to show the child who is "boss," responses which promote further irresponsibility and damage the child's fragile self-concept. There is only a genuine attempt to help children become competent, effective, and responsible.

My youngest daughter was two years old when my wife and I decided that we wanted to teach her responsibility rather than punish her. If our attempts to have her stop behaving unacceptably weren't quickly successful, Melanie would be told to go to her room until she could devise a plan to behave more responsibly. She was allowed to have fun, to be happy, to retain power and self-esteem by determining when she was going to plan behaviors that would lead to her being allowed to join the rest of the family. Generally, she would play in her room for awhile, until she decided it would be more satisfying to join the rest of us downstairs. It was then that she would appear at the top of the stairs and announce, "I have a plan." When questioned what her plan was, she would almost always say, "I'm coming down now!" To expect much more of a two year old would have been foolish, so Melanie would come downstairs and we would help her develop more specific, but age appropriate plans.

Effective discipline is not easy. It is easier to yell at or spank a misbehaving child than it is to take the time to help him develop a plan for more appropriate behavior. Punishment is especially attractive when young children seem to respond so well to its occasional use. The hectic, stressful environment of a classroom populated by young children can make the short-term relief provided by the use of punishment very alluring. Parents home with young children all day or those returning home after a hard day at work may find punishment an attractive quick-fix. But before you embrace the use of punishment, ask yourself these difficult questions: Is there a long-term negative consequence to my use of punishment? Will punishing this child help him/her? Will it help me get what I want in the long run? Can I choose a more effective behavior? One that will help the child grow, both cognitively and emotionally? One which will help the child make better decisions? One that will help the child become more responsible? One that will help me become more like the ideal teacher or parent I would like to be? My guess is that once you answer these questions, punishment will never again be as attractive as it has been, and you will become an advocate of the use of firm, strong discipline in your attempt to help children grow up responsibly.

Control Theory teaches us that we always have some control over what we do. Our lives, good or bad, happy or miserable, are largely the product of our choices. Control Theory stresses the concepts of freedom and responsibility. An unfortunate and unintentional by-product of a belief in stimulus-response theory is an abdication of personal responsibility. If I am taught that my actions are controlled by my parents' and teachers' use of punishment and rewards, I come to believe that my current life difficulties are not my fault (e.g., "Everything would be fine if my girlfriend would only pay more attention to what I'm saying." "The teachers in this school just don't know how to teach." "Gregory made me do it.") Stimulus-response theory unwittingly fosters the blaming and externalizing that characterize so many irresponsible people. Blaming, getting angry, feeling guilty or depressed may seem appropriate for a while, but none of these strategies helps to solve your difficulties in the long run. To live a more effective life and to be a happier person, you will have to act differently from how you are acting right now. That is a difficult discovery to make and one many of us hide from for years because it involves work; but it is also a powerful, exciting discovery, because along with the work comes the ultimate realization that you hold the key to your future happiness. You no longer have to look outside of yourself to find the road to a happier life. You are not at the mercy of your boss, your family, your government. Just as you must confront the fact that you are choosing whatever pain you are presently experiencing, you can take solace in the knowledge that you can make better choices beginning right now, and you can begin to choose happiness.

Developmental Appropriateness

Control Theory and Reality Therapy can be used successfully with people of any age, in any stage of development. However, the age and developmental level of your children has to be taken into consideration if you are to be effective in your use and teaching of Control Theory and Reality Therapy. The ideas and concepts presented in this book can be applied successfully with children as young as two years old, but only if the child's developmental level is taken into consideration and the process applied accordingly. It is perfectly appropriate for you to ask two year old children to think. It is perfectly appropriate for you to help two year old children see the connections among their behavioral choices, what happens to them, and their current level of happiness. Expecting two year olds to plan more effective behavior independently is folly. To ask young children to assume more responsibility than is developmentally possible will lead only to frustration, because it simply will not work. On the other hand, using these concepts within a developmentally appropriate context can help children learn to meet their needs in a more responsible fashion.

It is not my purpose to discuss developmental issues in any great detail. Most early childhood educators have had courses in child development and are experienced in working with children. They understand how children typically behave at certain ages and during certain stages of development. Many parents, even without formal training in child development, have a good sense of just what their child needs, how much stimulation is too much or too little, and what demands can be reasonably placed on their child. For those of you who feel that you would like more information in this area, the ideas of Arnold Gesell and Jean Piaget are particularly recommended. The "Suggestions for Further Reading" section at the end of this book offers titles of books you may find worth reading. The most important thing for you to remember is that children have special needs because of their age, their level of development, and their individuality. Keep this in mind as you implement the ideas presented in this book.

A Special Note To Classroom Teachers

While the primary focus of this book is to help children grow individually, the fact is that most of you work with groups of children. It is, therefore, critically important to develop skills which will lead to more effective functioning within the group as well. In order to promote optimum growth, teachers need to create an environment which encourages children to satisfy their four basic psychological needs (love, power, fun, freedom) on a regular basis. Remember that our behavior is an attempt to satisfy these needs and an environment in which these needs are consistently met fosters healthy development. Discipline problems will decrease in such a setting since children's needs will be met within child-initiated, teacher sanctioned activities. There will be less cause, therefore, for children to engage in inappropriate, disruptive behavior to meet their needs.

Think for a minute about some of the disruptive behavior you must deal with daily. Is it possible that the disruptive child is choosing that behavior in an attempt to meet his need for personal power? If so, remember that the child's need for power can't be turned off. If you were able to develop activities which would allow him to meet his need for power, his disruptive behavior would diminish significantly and you would both be a lot happier.

Take some time to think about the activities you currently use with your children and ask yourself this question: "What need or needs are addressed by this activity?" I'm willing to bet that every activity satisfies one or more of the four basic psychological needs. I will also bet that some activities satisfy more needs than others, and these are probably your most popular, successful activities. One key to building a successful educational program is making sure that the activities chosen by adults and children are diverse enough to address each of the four basic psychological needs on a daily basis, in a balanced way. Optimum growth and development can occur only in an environment where all four basic needs are met in a balanced way. If you offer a choice of activities with this premise in mind, you will be on your way to creating a more effective educational program.

Using This Book

In the following chapters I have adapted the concepts of Perry Good's *In Pursuit of Happiness* for your work with young children. Each chapter is divided into two sections: "Think It" and "Do It.". The first examines one of the Control Theory concepts covered in *In Pursuit of Happiness* and explains how that particular concept is relevant to the lives of young children. The second section of each chapter consists of age-appropriate activities for children so they can actually practice Control Theory and begin to learn how to choose happiness.

The initial activity for most chapters allows you to introduce the concept highlighted in that particular chapter by means of a conversation with a puppet. Children love puppets, and teachers are well aware of their educational value. Many of you, undoubtedly, already use puppets regularly in your programs. Parents can use puppets with children at home just as easily. As you introduce various Control Theory concepts, your children will attend longer and learn more because puppets help make learning fun.

For each of these introductory activities, I have provided a sample dialogue between you and "Do-It," a flying snail puppet. Patterned after Jeff Hale's illustration in Perry Good's book *In Pursuit of Happiness*, "Do-It" the flying snail is an unusually appealing, fanciful creature. With its cheerful colors, friendly expression and golden wings, it symbolizes happiness, love, power, fun and freedom—the essential concepts of this program. ("Do-It" puppets can be ordered from New View Publications, Box 3021, Chapel Hill, NC 27515.) If you do not have a "Do-It" puppet, use any other appealing puppet you do have, or fashion a simple puppet from an old sock by drawing features with colorful fabric markers, perhaps adding a couple of buttons for eyes. I cannot overemphasize that the dialogues are simply to guide you, to get you going, especially if you have not had many opportunities to use puppets in the past. Once you become more comfortable with the sense of the puppet dialogues, I am confident you will be developing your own, highly creative scripts.

The puppet activities are usually followed by "Happy Book" activities. Children, with adult help if needed, complete pages in the companion workbook, *I'm Learning To Be Happy* (available from New View Publications, as above). This individual work helps the children solidify their understanding of each concept as they create a very personal record of the program. Suggestions for additional activities of various sorts are also included in most of the chapters.

All of the activities included in Part II have been designed to be used with children three years old through the third grade. I have attempted to suggest activities which can be used both at home and in school, individually and in groups, by children at various stages of development. Some activities may be used more readily in given settings or with children of a particular age, but most of the activities can be easily adapted for your particular situation.

It would be nice if there were one "right" way to use this book, but a number of approaches are equally valid. You should read through the entire text before you begin to implement any of the ideas or activities with your children to be sure that you are fully acquainted with Control Theory. After a first reading, each of you will have to forge your own path. Some educators, for example, may want to base a one- or two-month unit of study on the ideas and activities presented here. One preschool teacher has told me she anticipates using this "total immersion" approach, at least as an initial introduction to Control Theory. She then expects to integrate a Control Theory orientation into her existing, successful program. Others may find that the material works into their current programs more comfortably if they use the activities once a week or one week a month. Parents, too, may find that particular approaches better suit certain children and families. In short, experiment to see which approach best fits you and your children.

For those of you who want more direction from the author, I will share my personal bias. For both parents and educators, I favor the "total immersion" approach as a first step. That is, I would move right through the book, using the activities in a systematic way to give the children an overall sense of what choosing happiness is all about. I would then return to specific concepts and activities on a regular basis to review what the children have learned. This second phase represents an on-going Control Theory approach to teaching and parenting which I believe helps children grow up to be happier and more responsible. As I said, however, my bias represents only one "right" way. I would be delighted to hear from any of you about other successful approaches you implement.

Before you begin Part II, consider for a moment what you are about to begin. You are about to help children learn specific ways to meet their needs more responsibly in an increasingly complex world. You are about to help children learn that they are largely in control of their own lives and their own happiness. You are about to help children learn that they are not controlled from the outside, but from within. You are preparing to provide your children with a gift that some others may never receive, that many receive only in adulthood: the knowledge that they can choose to lead happier, more productive lives regardless of their current life circumstances.

Ralph Waldo Emerson, wrote in "Nature,": "Good thoughts are no better than good dreams, unless they be executed!" Translated into Control Theory terms: "After you THINK IT, DO IT!"

PART II

TEACH THEM TO BE HAPPY

Introduction: Our Basic Needs

Too many of us think that we can achieve happiness by earning more money, by accumulating more things, or by waiting patiently for it to "happen" to us. Happiness, however, is achieved when we are able to satisfy our basic psychological needs in a balanced, varied way. Just as importantly, we can't simply will ourselves to feel happier. In order to be happier, to be more successful in our attempt to live our lives, we have to think and act. It's amazing how many of us seem to know this basic truth, yet fail to apply it regularly. When children feel sad, successful teachers and parents get them to do something different, to join the group, to play a game. The sadness usually disappears, replaced by happiness, the result of doing something more effective. Still, we continue to see feelings as separate from doing and thinking. Helping children make this connection is one of the major goals of this book.

Let's look at each of the basic needs in detail so we will develop an understanding of what they really are:

LOVE can be seen as friendship, as caring about others. One way to assess your own success in meeting your need for love is to consider all the people in your life and determine if there are people for whom you care deeply and who care deeply about you. Most of us have several people who fall into this category, but every one of us needs at least one person to whom we feel especially close. The same is true for children. Hopefully, most children feel loved by parents, grandparents, brothers, and sisters. Teachers can love their students, and it is a fact that most children feel a special fondness for their first teachers. Even less fortunate children however, need to love and be loved. For many of these children who may be victims of abuse, neglect or abandonment, the need to love and be loved may be difficult to satisfy because they lack the skills and behaviors which make them attractive to other children and to many adults. Their need, however, is just as strong. All children are born with the need to love and belong. Some simply have the need met more regularly and have developed more effective behaviors to satisfy that need. Our goal is to help all of the children we work with to meet their need for love, at least during the time they are in our care, whether that be in our schools or in our homes.

POWER is perhaps the most misunderstood of the basic needs because we tend to think of power in its most negative sense, power over other people. The power we are talking about, however, is personal power, a sense of competence, a sense that there are things I can do well. It involves recognition, an acknowledgment that what I do and who I am are important. Power often comes from other people, but it is important to realize that you always can congratulate yourself on a job well done. You can remind yourself daily that you are competent, that you have certain specific talents, that you are important. Far from being obnoxious and egotistical, self-appreciation helps to satisfy your need for power. The need for power is more difficult for children to satisfy, but it can be addressed by sensitive teachers and parents. Children can be praised daily for the things they do well. Most teachers routinely provide children with recognition when they engage in appropriate behavior and these comments help children meet their need for power: "That's a wonderful drawing, Jonathan!" "I like the way you and Sarah cooperated, Beth." "Good talking, Kevin. I like it when you use your words." etc. Also, children can participate regularly in short activities which involve giving recognition to classmates for skills they have displayed and by identifying skills and competencies within themselves. Similar activities can be done at home. Frequently at dinner, my wife and I will ask our three children to identify two things they did well that day. We stress the present because we want them to see that they demonstrate competence every day, not just on those special days when they have finally mastered some prized skill. Regular experiences such as these can help even very young children experience feelings of self-worth which are so critical to healthy development.

FUN was wonderfully defined by Mark Twain as "what you do when you don't have to do it." Most children are adept at having fun, playing as often as they can. Adults, generally, are less skillful and some even go so far as to see fun in negative terms ("It's childish behavior"). Perhaps most important for us is to recognize that there is an intimate connection between fun and learning. Watch children at play. They are constantly discovering, learning, and having fun. Whenever any of us, old or young, discovers something new, there is a sense of wonder, excitement, and fun that accompanies the learning. One of the saddest, self-defeating comments a teacher can make is, "We're not here to have fun; we're here to learn." If only more teachers knew that the two are not at odds; they are mutually supportive. Parents who wish to raise happy, inquisitive children should provide them with as many fun activities as possible. When your child is having fun, she is learning and she is satisfying one of her basic psychological needs.

17

FREEDOM involves the ability to make choices. We are fortunate to live in a society that gives us considerable freedom and most of us make countless choices every day. Almost all of us recognize the importance of making choices, and even those who have never heard of Control Theory talk about the value of giving children choices. Two things are especially important to keep in mind here. The first is to help children recognize that they do make many choices every day. Many of them choose what clothes to wear (or at least what socks to wear!). Many preschool programs have times in the day when children select from a variety of approved activities, another choice. Many elementary schools incorporate "free time" into their day, a time when children are given freedom, provided they engage in a worthwhile, educational activity. Some families offer children a choice of desserts, a choice of sandwich for lunch, etc. Children will be happier if they learn to appreciate that their need for freedom is regularly satisfied. Just as importantly, that recognition will make it easier for them to give up some freedom when that's necessary, too. There are times when children need to remain quiet, put toys away, clean an area of the room, listen to the teacher or parent. These "infringements" on freedom are tolerated much more easily by children who are aware of the many freedoms they do have every day. The second point about freedom that merits emphasis is that we often limit ourselves, making it very difficult to satisfy this need. You may know some children who fall into this category, unwilling or unable to let themselves go, to really experience life fully. In a very real way, these children are victims of self-imprisonment. As long as they limit themselves, they will frustrate their need for freedom and be unable to experience all of the happiness they otherwise could. You will be helping these children immensely if you can find a way to let them take some risks and more successfully meet their need for freedom.

To be truly happy we need to satisfy each of our four basic psychological needs regularly and in a balanced way. Sounds simple, right? It's not. If it were, we'd live in a far happier world. Take a look around you and find a child who doesn't seem to be particularly happy. As you consider his unhappiness, you will probably realize that he is not meeting one or more of his basic needs. Until he finds and uses more effective behaviors to meet his needs, the unhappiness will persist. Conversely, once he begins to use more effective behaviors, he will immediately begin to feel happier. It can't be overstated. Feelings are directly related to what a person chooses to do. If someone wants to feel happier, they will have to do something different from whatever they currently are doing.

Even though we all share the basic psychological needs of love, power, fun, and freedom, there are many different ways to satisfy these needs. That is part of what makes us all individuals. If Meghan has well developed fine motor skills, she may find cutting and pasting activities to be satisfying, helping her to meet her needs for fun and power. If Jordan's fine motor skills are not so well developed, cutting and pasting activities may be tortuous for him. Still, he is driven to satisfy the same needs, so he has to search for other behaviors that will be effective for him. If he has well developed gross motor skills and has a chance to play on the jungle gym, he will probably be able to meet his needs for power and fun that way. While the needs are the same for all of us, the behaviors we choose are a reflection of our individuality. What's important is that each of us discover the behaviors that work for us and to accept the behaviors chosen by others. The only "rule" is that the behaviors we choose should be responsible: they allow us to satisfy our needs without interfering with another's attempt to satisfy his or her needs. Just as only you can know what makes you happy, only I can know what makes me happy. We each need to find out what works for us and then do it!

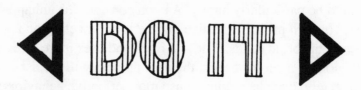

Ground Rules

Before beginning any activities, either at home or at school, it it wise to establish ground rules with the children. In fact, especially with younger children, it may be beneficial to begin each activity with a quick review of the behavioral expectations. The few minutes it takes to review the rules can set a positive tone and save a lot of unpleasant correcting of inappropriate behavior later on.

While each of you will need to develop guidelines which meet your specific circumstances, the following rules are pretty standard and can be used almost anywhere:

1. Children are expected to accept the choices and comments of the others in the group.
2. The group will not tolerate any negative feedback. If children believe their comments will be criticized, they will quickly learn that silence is the best policy and your group will not be successful.
3. Adults will have to be careful not to "edit" the choices made by children. If the children offer some inappropriate suggestions, take the opportunity to explore with them the consequences of their suggestion.

Activity #1: The Need for Love

Your first activity will introduce children to "Do-It", the flying snail puppet (or any other puppet character you choose) who will help them to learn how to live happier lives. In the initial activity, Do-It discusses the need for love and belonging.

What follows is a sample script. Feel free to modify it to suit your needs, style of speaking, and the developmental level of the child or children you are working with. The dialogue has

been written for group use, but it can be easily modified for a
single child simply by changing from plural to singular.

You: I have a friend I want you meet today. My friend is
named "Do-It," and Do-It has some interesting things to
tell us.

Do-It: Thanks. Hi, kids! It's great fun for me to get to visit
with you. I don't know if I've ever seen such a happy
group of kids before.

Y: Well, Do-It, that's one of the things we try to do here.
Have everyone be happy.

D: And that's just what I wanted to talk about with all of
you: some of the things that we need to make us happy.

Y: What do you mean, Do-It?

D: I mean we all need certain things to make us happy.
One of them is love. Everybody in the whole world
needs somebody they really love, somebody they really
care about. Somebody who really loves them and cares
about them. I bet the children have some people in their
lives they love. Can we ask them?

Y: Sure. (To the children): Can any of you tell Do-It someone you really love who loves you, too? Remember to
raise your hands.

At this point Do-It and the children can discuss various
people who help the children meet their need for love and
belonging. While Do-It and the children create a master list,
you can put all of the class contributions on a large piece of
newsprint or posterboard. This master list should be displayed
proudly in the room with the heading "People We Love."
Parents completing this activity at home with their children can

21

create a list to put on the wall or refrigerator. (While it is hardly the objective of this book, these activities are helpful pre-reading experiences for preschool children and will strengthen reading skills of elementary school children). Once the list has been completed, finish your dialogue with Do-It.

Y: Well, thanks, Do-It. I think we all had a good time and learned what makes us happy—love.

D: There's more to it than that, you know. If you'd like, I'd be glad to come back and talk about the other things we need to make us happy.

Y: That would be wonderful, Do-It. Why don't we plan to have you talk with us again soon. (Note: If at all possible, set a specific day and time when Do-It will talk with the children again.)

D: That sounds good to me. Thanks, kids! I'll look forward to talking to you again.

Activity #2: The Need for Power

In this dialogue, Do-It introduces the children to the need for power. With young children, I try not to use the word "power." It is confusing enough for adults and usually completely baffling to young children. Instead, ask the children to tell Do-It things they can do well, what they are proud of doing, or times when they feel important. Nearly all children are proud of something they do. It doesn't matter what children say as long as it represents something where they feel powerful or competent.

You: Good morning, Do-It. It's nice to see you again.

Do-It: Hi. Hi, kids. I hope all of you are happy this morning. Remember the other day we talked about how important it is to have people to love? Today, I want to talk about another thing we all need to be happy. I need your help again to make another list. O.K.?

Y: What should I do, Do-It?

D: You can help by writing down what we say, just like the last time. Hey, there's your other list! You left it up on the wall. That's great! Look at all those "People We Love."

Y: What's a good name for this list, Do-It?

D: Let's call this one "Things We Do Well." I bet everybody here does some things very well. We need to know that we can be successful, that there are things we do well, in order to be happy. It makes us feel good to know we're good at some things, even if we can't do everything. Can any of you you tell me something you do well, something you're proud of doing?

Follow the procedure you used in the activity for love, accepting all suggestions and creating a master list. When finished, end your conversation with Do-It, making plans to have another conversation soon about the other things we need to make us happy.

Activity #3: The Need for Freedom

In this dialogue, Do-It introduces the children to the need for freedom. Children will probably have some difficulty understanding the concept of freedom, so Do-It will talk to them about choices. You could begin by listing choices that we make at home, in school, etc., to get the group going. As soon as someone mentions "I picked out this shirt," you'll quickly have a large list of choices children make and they'll see, perhaps for the first time, that they do many things that give them freedom. Even for children unable to read, there is something powerful and liberating about a wall hanging that an-

23

nounces "Choices We Make."

You: Do-It. We're glad to see you.

Do-It: And I'm glad to see all of you again. I hope that all of you have been making sure you have been doing things that make you happy.

Y: We've been trying our best. You said you had even more things you wanted to talk about with us.

D: That's right. There are still two more important things we need if we really want to be happy.

Y: Two more? What are they?

D: Well, today I just want to talk about one. Today I want to talk about choices.

Y: What do you mean "choices"?

D: Well, to be really happy, you have to have some freedom. You have to be able to make some choices.

Y: What kinds of choices?

D: Just choices. I bet you give the kids some choices here. (To the kids.) Is that true? Who can tell me about some of the choices you have here? (To the adult) Will you write this down for us?

Y: Sure, Do-It. What do you want to call this list?

D: How about "Choices We Make"? O.K., kids. Let's hear about some of the choices you make.

24

At the conclusion of this activity, make plans for Do-It to come back to discuss the remaining basic need, fun.

Activity #4: The Need for Fun

In this activity, Do-It will talk with the children about the things they do for fun. The need for fun will probably be the easiest to discuss. Children are usually good at having fun and can identify what they do for fun. Probably the greatest problem you will face here will be children who make critical comments about another child's selection. This is especially true with older children who are much more selective and judgmental about which activities are fun and which activities are not. Remember the ground rules. You may want to stress with your group that all suggestions are "right" for the person who made them, that it's O.K. for them to disagree, but that they don't need to voice their disagreement. With most children, as long as their ideas are given recognition (power), they are willing to be tolerant of someone else's idea of fun. Once the list has been generated, your wall can be decorated with a poster that tells everyone "Things We Do For Fun."

You: Good morning, Do-It.

Do-It: Good morning. Hi, everybody. Boy, am I excited today.

Y: How come?

D: Today, I get to talk with you about the other thing we need in order to be happy. We have already talked about having people to love, of having things we can do well, and being able to make some choices.

Y: What else is there?

D: The other thing everybody needs is fun! Does everybody here like to have fun? Hey, let's make another list. We can call it "Things We Do For Fun."

25

Y: O.K., Do-It. I have paper to make a list. Remember, children, to raise your hands and listen to everybody else so we can all enjoy this activity.

D: Let's begin. Who would like to tell me something they do that's fun?

Again, create a master list of activities, making sure that each child has an opportunity to contribute if they choose to.

Y: Well, Do-It, I want to thank you for coming and telling us about all the things we need in order to be happy.

D: It has been my pleasure. I like helping people learn about what they need to be happy. It makes it easier to be happy if you know what you need to be happy.

Y: I think I know what you mean. Well, Do-It, this is kind of sad. I think we're all going to miss you around here.

D: I could come back if you want. I still have lots more to share with you and the kids. And being with all of you is one of the things I do to make me happy. Would it be O.K. if I came back again sometime?

Y: Do-It, I think that would be wonderful. What do you think, children? It sounds like they'd like to see you, too, Do-It.

D: Great. I'll be here when you need me. Bye for now, kids!

Children at home or in school can decorate the posters they

have made with drawings depicting how they meet their needs.

Activities # 5-8: Happy Book Activities

These four follow-up activities ("People I Love," "Things I Do Well," "Choices I Make," and "Things I Do For Fun") are designed for children to complete individually, with your help. The follow-up activities allow the children to reflect upon what they have discussed with Do-It. By completing these activities, children will solidify their understanding of the basic psychological needs.

Once the children have completed generating master lists for each of the four basic needs, they are ready to make their own individual lists. The activity pages which comprise *I'm Learning To Be Happy*, a companion to this book, are designed for individual children to record their own answers for each of the group activities offered here, creating a personal memory album as they are introduced to these concepts. Notice that for each activity, there are three spaces for each basic need. I have included only three lines so that children won't feel bad if they are unable to fill up the entire page. After completing the group activity with Do-It, however, each child should be able to list three people or activities for each of the basic needs. Let them keep going, though, if they want to include more.

Most children are going to need adult assistance to complete their *I'm Learning To Be Happy* books. Many of them will be unable to read or write, so an adult will have to help them by reviewing the group list and letting them choose what they want to include in their individual books. It's critically important that children be allowed to choose what they want. We may think they should include family members on the "Love and Belonging" page, whereas they may choose friends. Don't edit their choices. If they get the idea that there are "right" and "wrong" answers, they will quickly develop strategies to figure out what answers you want them to provide (to help them satisfy their need for love and belonging), and the activities will have far less real value and meaning.

You should feel free to adapt all of the activities in this

27

LOVE

People I Love

1._____

2._____

3._____

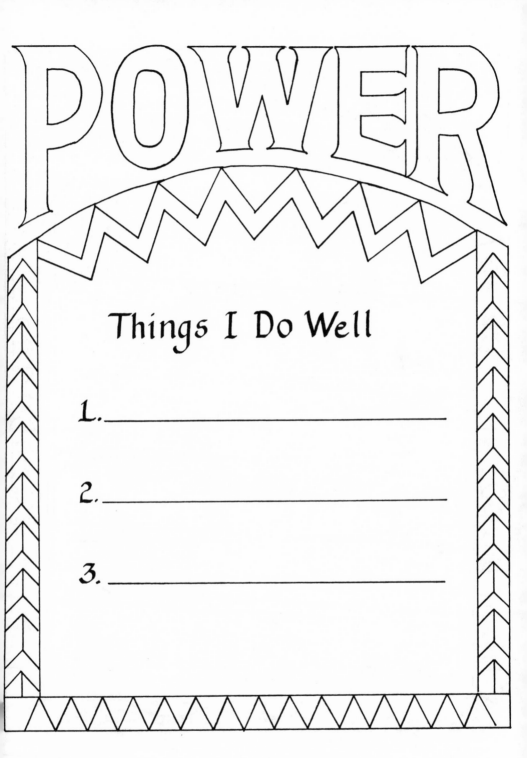

POWER

Things I Do Well

1. _____

2. _____

3. _____

FREEDOM

Choices I Make

1. _____

2. _____

3. _____

FUN

Things I Do For Fun

1._____

2._____

3._____

31

You should feel free to adapt all of the activities in this book to fit the needs of the children you serve. In general, however, you will probably find the introductory activities with Do-It to be good energizers, while the completion of the *I'm Learning To Be Happy* books are much better suited for quiet times and can be done later in the day. Regardless, if at all possible, you should try to end each activity with some type of discussion about the importance of what the children have done. Let them know, in language that they can understand, that these things are the keys to being happy and that together you are going to learn how to be happy as often as possible. While they may not be able to grasp fully everything you are trying to tell them, you will be getting children to think, an important goal in itself. Just as importantly, you will get them to start thinking that there may be a way for them to create more happy moments in their lives. That's a possibility that most of us, young and old, will gladly spend time considering.

Activity #9: Photo Album (Love)

Have the child tell you the names of some people he loves. If this activity is done in a school setting and the child mentions some classmates, take pictures of those classmates. Gather together some photographs of people the child has mentioned and glue the pictures onto paper, forming a book. Staple the pages together and on the front include the title "People I Love" and the author's name.

Activity #10: Pictures of Success (Power)

At school or at home, take pictures of something a child has done particularly well and make a bulletin board with Pictures of Success. (Example: Jodi standing next to a block building she has constructed.) Educators, be certain that every child has the opportunity for his or her Picture of Success to be on the bulletin board regularly.

Chapter One: Signals

This chapter is about signals, those vital messages that let us know whether or not we are meeting our needs. Every one of us knows, at every moment, just how we want our world to be at that particular time. We have a mental "picture" of how we can satisfy our basic needs now. At the same time, our senses and perceptions are monitoring what is going on in the real world. These two images are being constantly compared. If the real world seems to be like the picture I have in my head at that moment, I get a positive signal. If the real world seems to be different from how I would like it to be, I get a negative signal. Signals are vital. Without signals, we wouldn't know if we were meeting our needs, and without that knowledge we wouldn't know if we were happy or sad.

Signals last only an instant and are internal. In the strictest sense, we aren't even consciously aware of them. They are just felt as an urge to behave, to continue a behavior that's getting us a positive signal or to change behaviors if we're getting a negative signal. The interval between receiving a signal and behaving is nearly imperceptible, especially in young children. Just watch young children for a while and you'll soon be given a glimpse of their internal signals. When children are engaging in satisfying behaviors, their brains are pumping out positive signals and the children are driven to sustain that behavior. That's why children, despite their limited attention span, will sometimes spend long periods of time engaging in a particular activity and become visibly upset when they are told that it is time to stop doing something they are enjoying. Their signals are telling them to continue the satisfying behavior and we are telling them it's time to stop. The same can be said of negative signals. When young children are not meeting their needs, they feel a negative signal and almost immediately act upon it, making us aware, through their behavior, that their needs are not satisfied. They will yell, hit, throw things, sulk, have a tantrum, switch activities, or engage in any other behavior they think has a reasonable chance of helping them more success-fully meet their needs. While each of us has our own individual system of signals, signals always function to let us know if we are meeting our basic needs.

The more you become sensitive to and aware of your sig-nals, both positive and negative, the more you will be able to truly understand how happy you are. As elementary as it sounds, one of the first steps in improving your level of happi-ness is to figure out just where you are now. Recognizing your signals will help you immensely.

Of course, not all signals are equally strong. A child mo-mentarily unable to locate her mother experiences a negative signal that is jolting in its strength. There is a massive discrep-ancy between the information coming in and the picture she has in her head of how the world should be. Once she locates her mother, walking towards her with open arms, an equally strong positive signal sweeps over her and bathes her in mo-mentary, but pure ecstasy. Most other signals are far less extreme. Our days are characterized by minor triumphs and minor annoyances, each producing signals, but most of us are less adept at identifying these important markers. In many ways these minor signals are just as important as the louder signals because a major portion of our overall happiness is determined by routine, everyday events. Most young children can tell you why their birthday party was a success ("Everybody gave me presents!" "We got to eat cake and ice cream!" "All my friends were there!"), but it takes much more skill and effort to tell what made a more ordinary day a success. It takes considerable practice to recognize and act effectively on the minor signals we get every waking hour of every day, but it is worth the effort because it enriches our lives.

It's funny how quickly we attend to the physical signals tied to survival, while many of us ignore the psychological signals tied to happiness. When we get a "hunger" signal, we do something. We eat. When we get a "cold" signal, we do something. We put on a sweater. Too many of us, however, try to ignore the psychological signals even when we recognize them. Why? For many, it is simply because we don't know what to do when we recognize the "angry," "depressed," or "scared" signals. So we try to ignore them, hoping they'll just go away. The problem is, they don't. Signals are messengers and they won't go away until the message has been delivered, and as far as the signals are concerned, the message hasn't been delivered until you do something. The message is always the same: you don't have enough love, power, fun, or freedom in your life right now. To get enough and to get rid of the negative signal, you'll have to do something different.

Once you acknowledge a negative signal, you have to take the responsibility for doing something to help you get what you want. In a very real way, if you don't choose to do something different, you are choosing the misery you will continue to experience. That's a difficult concept for many people to accept. They find it easier to blame their feelings, especially their miserable ones, on other people ("You make me so angry!"). But other people don't make us anything. We receive the negative signal that the world is not the way we want it right now, that our needs are not being satisfied, and we choose anger, or depression, or guilt, etc., because at that moment we believe it will satisfy our needs. When my son, Gregory, misbehaves, he doesn't make me angry. I receive a negative signal, then I choose anger because I believe that showing anger will help me get what I want. It usually works, in the short run. Greg's need for love and belonging is such that usually he will then choose to behave in a way that I define as appropriate. The questions all of us who deal with young children have to ask ourselves are: (1) Are there long-term negative consequences to choosing anger regularly in order to get what we want? and (2) What other, more effective behaviors could we choose when we receive negative signals?

Many people would rather blame their feelings and behaviors on others. Some simply don't want to do the hard work of getting what they want in a responsible way. Some people feel that no matter what they do, they won't get what they want anyway. If you find yourself in one of these categories, you'll have to give up these attitudes if you really want to live a happier life. Becoming responsible for your own happiness may be tough, but it's necessary if you want to be happy.

Recognizing Positive Signals

Our brain has developed to help us survive. It is no surprise, therefore, that we are much better at recognizing negative signals than positive ones. While this may be advantageous for survival, it doesn't do much to make us happy. If we want to be happier, we have to do a better job of recognizing when we are getting what we want.

One thing which distinguishes happy people from unhappy people is that happy people are more aware of what they are doing right and when they are doing something that helps them meet their needs. This insight helps them savor life more completely. Children must become more aware of just what they are doing when they are receiving positive signals and feeling happy. We can assist by helping them make the connection between the behavior they are currently choosing and the good feeling they are experiencing. I frequently do this with my children. Their facial expressions tell me that they are receiving powerful positive signals at that moment. So that they won't make the common mistake of believing that happiness just "happened" to them, I ask them what they are doing. I then ask them how they are feeling. Over time, they will make the connection between doing and feeling and learn that they can voluntarily choose from a repertoire of behaviors which will help them experience happiness on a regular basis.

Recognizing Negative Signals

We are pretty good at recognizing negative signals, especially the loud ones. If you want to be happier, however, you'll have to start becoming aware of and doing something about the quieter negative signals you tend to ignore. Ignoring negative signals would be effective if the signals just went away, but they don't. In fact, ignored signals can lead to headaches, backaches, ulcers, general sickness, chronic fatigue, and other symptoms. An example will probably make this concept easier to understand. Tommy, a second grade student, is in the low reading group in his class and his classmates frequently make fun of his poor academic performance. Every morning, when it's time to go to school, he gets a negative signal. He knows, as young as he is, that school is not a satisfying place for him. His need for love is certainly unmet there, as well as his need for power since he is not as academically skilled as his peers. Obviously, Tommy is not having much fun at school. He tells his parents that he doesn't want to go to school, but their answer is simply that he must go. This certainly doesn't help

Tommy satisfy his need for freedom. The negative signal is still going off loudly, urging him to try new behaviors to get what he wants. He tries crying and throws a tantrum, behaviors that have been effective in the past. A power struggle with his parents ensues, but they still tell him that he must go to school. Tommy may give up the struggle, trying to ignore the signal, but as long as his needs are not being met, the signal will continue to work on Tommy. Soon, Tommy becomes sick. Now he can't go to school. Because his sickness is not seen as a choice, Tommy gets lots of love, understanding, and support from his parents. One of them may even have to stay home from work to be with Tommy, providing Tommy with an unexpected measure of power. Tommy is not being manipulative. He really is sick. If he were faking, he would likely be discovered easily and sent to school. No one, including Tommy, realizes that the unaddressed negative signal still drives him to behave in an effort to satisfy his needs. The signal doesn't care if the behavior he chooses is responsible. It doesn't care if the behavior he chooses is harmful. Its job is simply to activate his system so that he will behave in an effort to satisfy his needs. Becoming sick is much more satisfying to Tommy than going to school, and until Tommy can find a better way to meet his needs in school, he will continue to be sick. There are thousands, maybe millions of children like Tommy who go through our public school system this way, missing enormous time from school. Most of them are completely unaware that their chronic inability to attend school is a creative behavior they have developed to help them meet their needs.

If we want to keep our negative signals from becoming subversive and leading us into psychosomatic illness, we would be well advised to pay attention to them as soon as possible. Further, we should practice recognizing negative signals before they get out of hand. We can train ourselves and our children to see negative signals more favorably. We can choose to see a child who is throwing a tantrum, not as a behavior problem, but as a person experiencing a negative signal, a person trying to meet his needs, and we can help that child develop more effective, responsible behaviors. Negative signals are, after all, only messages that we are not getting what we want. That message, if acted upon effectively and responsibly, can be a catalyst in our decision to live happier lives.

Although it is difficult to teach the complex, abstract concept of signals to young children because they lack cognitive maturity, it is easy to recognize signals in children. As adults, we become quite skilled at masking our signals, and other people frequently are unable to read them in our body language or on our faces. Also, as we mature we choose more unique, individual patterns of behavior. You and I may both experience the same signal, but show it in very different, subtle ways. Young children, on the other hand, are more overt and demonstrative, less individualized. Most preschoolers and primary grade students who experience strong positive signals show it in their faces immediately. Many of them get their whole bodies involved in the celebration, clapping, jumping, and laughing. Young children are just as quick to make us aware when they have received negative signals. Crying, yelling, foot-stomping, and sulking are common behaviors among young children who have received negative signals. So while young children may have difficulty fully grasping the concept of signals, they can be taught to recognize the behaviors that quickly follow signals, both in themselves and in others.

The first goal, then, is to teach children to recognize the behavioral symptoms that accompany signals. The long range goal is to have children see that these behaviors are being chosen in an attempt to satisfy needs and that other behaviors could be chosen, too. Put simply, while we don't choose the signal, we do choose what to do after we receive the signal.

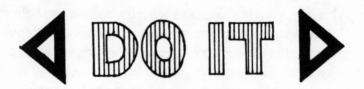

Recognizing Positive Signals

Activity #1: Positive Signals

In this activity, Do-It will introduce the concept of positive signals to children. Don't be surprised or alarmed if your children are unable to generate a particularly long list for this activity. Since young children are still many years away from fully developing their individuality, their answers may represent a fairly narrow spectrum of behaviors. As they get older, individual differences will become increasingly apparent. Here's a sample dialogue for you to use to have Do-It introduce Positive Signals to children.

You: (Keeping Do-It out of sight.) Do-It? Oh, Do-It? Where are you? You said you'd be here when we wanted you. Do-It?

Do-It: (Popping up) Here I am! Just like I promised. It's important to do what you say you'll do. Hey, look at all those happy faces. That's just what I wanted to talk about.

Y: Happy faces?

D: Kind of. Remember when we talked before about what you need to be happy?

Y: Sure. Do you children remember?

Here you should review very briefly the basic needs (love, power, freedom, and fun) if it seems appropriate.

40

D: My question for you now is, "How do we know when we're happy? How do we look? How could you tell, just by looking at someone, that they were happy?"

Y: I have an idea. Why don't we make another list. I've got some paper right here. Who wants to give Do-It some ideas about how we know when we're happy?

Record responses while Do-It interacts with the children. If younger children have some difficulty, Do-It can ask such questions as: How do you look when you are happy? How do you feel when you get what you want? How does your body feel when you're happy? How can you tell, just by looking at them, when someone else in the group is happy? How did I know, just by looking at you, that you were happy to see me?

At the conclusion of the activity, make plans to have Do-It come again.

Activity #2: A Happy Book Activity

After completing the activity with Do-It, with adult assistance children can complete the page in their *I'm Learning To Be Happy* book headed "I Know When I'm Happy ."

While the formal activities about recognizing positive signals are themselves valuable, the real key to making this experience worthwhile is the regular follow-up provided by teachers and parents. First, practice being a model for the children. Regularly tell them about how you feel and how your feelings are related to what you are doing. Secondly, each day, when you see children meeting their needs you should ask them questions such as, "How do you know you're happy?" Children will then have the opportunity to recognize the positive signals that flood them when their needs are being met. They will start to notice their smiles, their relaxed bodies, their faces free of tension. Ideally, you will help children make connections between their happiness and their satisfied needs: "I'm smiling because I'm playing with Billy and having fun," "I'm clapping because I got it right!"

41

I Know When I'm Happy

I know I'm happy when

1. _____

2. _____

3. _____

People who know they are happy automatically become happier. I make it a point to bring my children's happiness to their attention every day. I then help them identify the behaviors they have chosen. The connections they make between their behavior and their happiness makes it much more likely that they will be happy again soon. Happiness no longer is seen as something that just happens to them. They know both when they are happy and what they did to be happy.

Recognizing Negative Signals

Activity #3: Negative Signals

In this activity, Do-It introduces the children to the concept of Negative Signals.

Do-It: Hi, everybody. Today I want to talk about something that's not so much fun. In fact, it's kind of sad.

You: Why, Do-It? I thought you visited us so that we could learn to be happier.

D: I do. But knowing when you're not happy is important if you want to be happy.

Y: I don't understand, Do-It. How can it help us to know we're sad? There's nothing we can do about it.

D: I'm not so sure about that. But we'll talk more about that another day. The point is, if you want to be happier, you have to know when you're not happy enough.

Y: I'm still not sure I understand.

D: That's O.K. This one is a tough one for grown-ups. The kids can probably help you understand. Why don't you get some paper. We're going to make another list. This

time, kids, I want you to finish this sentence: "I know
I'm sad when..."

If children experience difficulty, have Do-It ask them
questions such as: How do you look when you are sad? How
do you feel when you don't get what you want? How can you
tell, just by looking, when another child is sad? After the list
has been completed, continue your dialogue with Do-It.

Y: So what good is all of this, Do-It? How does knowing
        this help make us happier?

D: Well, these things we've written down are just signals.

Y: Signals?

D: Yeah, signals, telling us we're not getting what we
        need.

Y: So?

D: Well, a lot of the time, what we're doing isn't helping
        us get what we want. Like suppose someone took
        something you were playing with. What would you do?

Y: I might cry or look sad.

D: That's right. You get a signal that you're not happy, and
        then you do something like cry or look sad.

Y: But crying or looking sad doesn't usually help me get
        my things back.

D: That's right again. That's why whenever you get one of
        those negative signals you should stop and figure out
        what's wrong and then plan to do something that will
        get you what you need.

Y: It sounds pretty tough to me.

D: It is. But we've got lots of time. For now, I just want you and the kids to practice recognizing both positive and negative signals. And we'll talk more later.

Y: O.K., Do-It. We'll practice recognizing our signals. See you soon.

What is most important in this activity is that you and Do-It help the children to see that these behaviors can alert them that they aren't meeting their needs. Think about why children typically cry, have tantrums, or otherwise show their unhappiness. Isn't it always related to some need being frustrated? "They won't let me play with them" (love and belonging); "She took my block" (power); "I don't want to play that game" (freedom); "Can't we go down the slide one more time? Please?" (fun).

Your goal is to have crying children say (or at least understand), "I'm getting a signal." At that point you can intervene and help them figure out a better way to get what they want. Once they realize that negative signals are trying to tell them something, even young children can begin to figure out how to behave more effectively. The cognitive benefit to this is that you are helping children overcome their tendency to behave impulsively. Instead of simply crying and continuing in their misery, you have introduced children to the idea that the crying is a message that they need to do something better to meet their needs. That information alone is empowering and will considerably help many children to behave more effectively and responsibly.

45

Activity #4: A Happy Book Activity

After discussing Negative Signals with Do-It, children can complete, with adult assistance, the page in their *I'm Learning To Be Happy* book headed "I Know When I'm Sad."

Activity #5: Mirror, Mirror!

This delightful group activity can be done just as easily at home with one child.

Have the children sit in a circle. Pass around a hand mirror and ask each child to make a "happy face," "sad face," "angry face," etc. Discuss with the children what behaviors they are doing when they feel happy, sad, etc.

Activity #6: The Plate's The Thing!

Again, this activity can be done equally well with a single child or as a group. Give each child three plain white paper plates, and ask the children to draw a different face on each plate—one happy face, one sad and one angry. Then describe common situations and ask the children to hold up the plate that would represent the way they would feel. A discussion about the specific behaviors that accompany happiness, sadness, and anger could be included, geared to the developmental level of the children involved.

I Know When I'm Sad

I know I'm sad when

1._____

2._____

3._____

Chapter Two: Pictures

For each one of our basic needs, we have specific mental pictures or ideas of how we can satisfy that need. Each one of us develops our pictures individually, so mine will probably be different from yours.

While basic needs are universal, pictures are reflections of our individuality and are, in part, determined by our developmental level. A child's pictures might be something like these, developed by my son Greg, age five:

Love: Me and my Dad are at a baseball game.
Power: I hit a ball real far and get a home run.
Freedom: I decide what I want to do, like go to the park and play with my friends.
Fun: I am playing pirates or something like that with Kevin.

Throughout this book, we have spoken of wants. Essentially, wants are pictures and are always related to our basic psychological needs. You may be wondering how we get our pictures. Are we born with them? Are they inherited? Does everybody have pictures? It's probably easiest to begin by saying that, yes, everybody has pictures. Some of us have more than others, but every one of us must have at least one picture of how we can satisfy each of our basic psychological needs. That doesn't mean that we can achieve the picture, that the picture is good for us, or that our pictures aren't in conflict with each other. Still, despite these potential trouble spots, we all have pictures.

We aren't born with pictures. We are born with needs, but virtually no idea about how to satisfy them. As infants, we don't even have many behaviors we can perform voluntarily. Over time, however, certain behaviors we choose satisfy one or more of our basic needs and we store away the accompanying experiences. As we get older, we add to our collection of pictures, each one a memory of a satisfying experience or something we believe would be satisfying.

Let's look at a couple of examples. Sarah, six months old, is alone in her crib and gets a negative signal, meaning her needs are not being met. Like all infants, Sarah has very few behaviors she can voluntarily choose to meet her needs. One of the behaviors available to everyone at birth, and it's critically important to healthy development, is crying. With little else to choose from, Sarah begins to cry. Within minutes, perhaps seconds, her mother comes in, picks her up, and comforts her. Sarah quiets down and is a much happier infant. Sarah, as young as she is, puts a picture in her tiny album of being held by her mother, a picture of satisfying her need for love and belonging that will probably stay there forever. While Sarah may not have a great many sophistocated cognitive skills, you can be sure the event was significant enough that when she gets another negative signal in the near future, she'll most likely choose to cry because it was effective in helping her meet her need for love and belonging.

Of course, no behavior, even crying, is effective all of the time. When a behavior isn't effective, the negative signal continues to sound, and we search for other behaviors we have used successfully in the past or we create new behaviors to meet our present needs. That's why, over time, Sarah will learn to satisfy her needs with behaviors other than crying. When those new behaviors produce a satisfying experience, that experience, too, will become a picture for Sarah.

While we must have at least one picture of how we can satisfy each basic need, most of us have many. The more pictures that we can develop, the happier we'll be, because sometimes we just can't have the picture that we most want at that particular time. By having other pictures available, however, we still can find ways to meet our needs. Today my son Greg told me that he had wanted to play in the park with Kevin, but they couldn't because it was raining. Going to the park with Kevin was a picture he had in his head to satisfy the needs of love and fun. By having other pictures available, however, Greg was still able to meet his needs. He and Kevin played 'investigator' with his magnifying glass, and then later they played pirates. New pictures were substituted to meet the same basic needs.

All of our pictures together make up our ideal world. They represent how we would like our lives to be if we could have everything that we want. This is, however, very different from what we really need. We must satisfy our basic needs in order to be happy, but we don't have to satisfy them with any particular pictures. My three year old daughter, Melanie, needs love and has the picture of being with her mother in her album. If Melanie is at school, however, she'll find another picture to meet the need for love, probably including the teacher or perhaps a favorite classmate.

Birthdays are times when many of us, including children, have very definite pictures of how our needs would be satisfied. Talking ahead of time about everyone's pictures is a good way to avoid much of the disappointment and conflict that can mar these occasions. Discussing pictures ahead of time and working things out in advance also helps us determine which pictures are really important and which ones we are willing to give up. A child may want to invite "everybody" to his birthday party. By telling him ahead of time that he can invite any five friends he wants, he has time to redevelop his picture and decide which of his friends are most important. As painful as these choices may be, the processes of discrimination and decision-making are very helpful as children come to understand their emerging value systems. If we, as adults, want to help children become effective decision-makers, we must provide them with opportunities to make decisions when they are young.

Remember, pictures are not necessarily good for you in the long run, or even in the short run. Many children would prefer to eat candy instead of fruit, but we all know the different nutritional values of the two. Many children have a picture of watching TV in their heads and might do little else if not restricted by their parents. It is very difficult for children, who live in the present, to consider the long-range implications of their behavior. That's where you, as a need-satisfying adult, become very important. If you become a picture in their album, they are more likely to listen to you and accept fruit instead of candy, or play outside instead of watch TV, or share instead of act selfishly, or wait their turn instead of talk out. Of course, it won't work all the time, but you can help children develop healthier pictures if you make yourself a need-satisfying person in their lives.

Unfortunately, pictures are not always compatible. This morning Greg was meeting his need for power or competence as he built various things with his blocks. He gets lots of recognition for the creative buildings he constructs. As soon as he was told that Kevin wanted him to come over to his house and play, a picture of being with his friend came into focus, which presented an opportunity to satisfy Greg's needs for love and fun. The two pictures could not be achieved simultaneously. A conflict, albeit minor, had to be resolved, so the blocks were put away for another time. Through this process of resolving conflicts and making decisions, we develop our individual value systems that dictate, to a significant degree, how we choose to live our lives and what we will do in order to create happiness.

It is valuable to know just what your pictures are because they repesent what you really want. Wanting something doesn't mean you will get it, of course; but if you can identify what you want and tell others what that is, you have a better chance of getting most of what you want as well as what you need. Here is where teachers and other adults can be especially helpful to children. Remember that pictures relate to basic needs. When a child identifies a picture that he has, something he really wants, he's actually telling you what basic need or needs he wants to satisfy. Even if the picture he gives you is outlandish and can't be satisfied right now, you can still determine what needs the picture is designed to satisfy and help the child find other behaviors, and develop other, more realistically attainable pictures, to satisfy those needs.

If you want children to be really happy, you have to help them find what they want and develop behaviors that will turn those pictures into reality. Since many children have wants which can't be satisfied in the immediate future (e.g., "I want to be a Mommy," "I want to be on TV," etc.), focus on wants which they can satisfy in the present. For example, we may say, "You can pretend you are a Mommy and do the things a Mommy would do," or "We can get a video camera and you can practice what you want to do on TV." We are not trying to rob children of their dreams. Their long-range goals are critical components in their healthy development. Still, our immediate objective is to help children learn the process of choosing effective behaviors which will turn pictures into reality, and that process is more easily learned if we concentrate on more realistic, easily obtained pictures. The success children experience now will serve as a model to help them with the bigger, long-range wants we all have.

Just as we have to recognize positive signals if we want to be happier, we would do well to pay more attention to the many things we do have. Many adults fail to notice all the things they do well, all the effective behaviors they use to achieve many of the pictures in their personal picture albums. They constantly put more pressure on themselves, never believing they can let down and relax. Most of us don't want to saddle our children with this psychological burden, so it is important that we help them learn to appreciate all the things they do well which help them get what they want and experience that wonderful feeling we call happiness.

More than in some of the other chapters, the activities that are offered below involve considerable discussion. Young children need to be active and can only focus on discussions for short periods of time. Recognizing this, you may want to break these, or any other activities suggested in this book, into smaller segments that can be spread over several days. It is not necessary to do an entire activity in one sitting, or even in one day. In fact, as a general rule, children profit from lots of repetition. Consequently, it makes sense to spread activities out over a period of time to maximize their effectiveness. In all cases, use your judgment and move on to something else when you notice that the children are losing their ability to profit from a discussion. Remember, we are trying to help children make the connection between behavior and happiness. They won't be able to do that very well without giving the activities their attention and having fun.

Noticing What You Have

Activity #1: What We Have That Makes Us Happy
In this activity, Do-It will help the children recognize all the things they have that make them happy.

You: So, Do-It, what have you got planned for us today?

Do-It: Well, I've been doing a lot of thinking about this happiness thing.

Y: Yes, and what have you found?

D: It seems to me that the happiest people are more aware of all the things they have.

Y: What do you mean "aware"?

D: I mean they notice and appreciate all the things they do have instead of just complaining about what they don't have.

Y: And you think that makes people happier?

D: I'm sure of it. Everybody here has things that make them happy. Can we make another list?

Y: Sure. Let me reach over here and get the paper. Should we call it "What We Have That Makes Us Happy"?

D: Yes, that sounds good. Why don't you start us off with an example of something you have that makes you happy.

Y: O.K. I have friends. That makes me happy.

D: Good. Put that on our list. How about you kids? Let's hear some of the things you have that make you happy.

As Do-It and the children generate a list, you record their answers. At the completion of the activity, make plans to have Do-It come again soon.

Since children tend to be very materialistic, you or Do-It might offer one or two ideas like "my family" or "my friends," but don't be alarmed if the children's list is disproportionately materialistic. That's probably simply a reflection of their developmental level. What's important here is that children learn to be appreciative. If they can begin to learn that skill, then when they are older and more idealistic, they will come to appreciate some of the more abstract things we cherish in our culture.

Activity #2: What We Have Done Right & What That Means

In this activity, Do-It will help children realize they have done many things right and have many positive qualities.

You: What are we going to do today to make us happy?

Do-It: Oh, I like that. "What are we going to do?" I think you're starting to learn that how happy we are depends on what we choose to do.

Y: So what's today's activity?

D: I thought it would be fun to spend some more time talking about some of the things we already have.

Y: So we're going to do the same activity we did last time?

D: Not exactly. This time I want the kids to help me make a list called "What We Have Done Right and What That Means."

Y: Can you give us an example? Some of the children look a little confused.

D: Sure. This is a tough activity. I met a kid once who told me "I learned to play Candy Land. That means I'm smart."

Y: I get it. Another child once told me, "I helped my Dad

55

clean the kitchen. That means I'm a good helper."

D: That's a perfect example. Why don't we put those two
       on our list and now we'll hear from the kids. Who's got
       a good one for us to put on the list?

After the children have completed their list, make plans to
have Do-It visit again soon.

Activities #3 & 4: Happy Book Activities

The children can use the lists generated in Activities #1 &
#2 to help them complete the appropriate pages in their *I'm
Learning To Be Happy* books. ("What I Have That Makes Me
Happy" and "What I Have Done Right & What That Means."

Deciding What You Want

Activity #5: What We Want

Do-It will help the children create a list headed "What We
Want." Let the children use their imaginations, but encourage
some realistic, easily obtained wants.

You: Good morning, Do-It. What have you got planned for
       us today?

Do-It: Dreaming.

Y: Dreaming?

D: Yup. We've been talking about all the things we have.
       Today, let's make a list of some things we would like to
       have that we don't yet have.

Y: You mean like a new bike?

WHAT I HAVE THAT MAKES ME HAPPY

1.＿＿＿＿＿＿＿＿＿＿＿＿＿＿＿

2.＿＿＿＿＿＿＿＿＿＿＿＿＿＿＿

3.＿＿＿＿＿＿＿＿＿＿＿＿＿＿＿

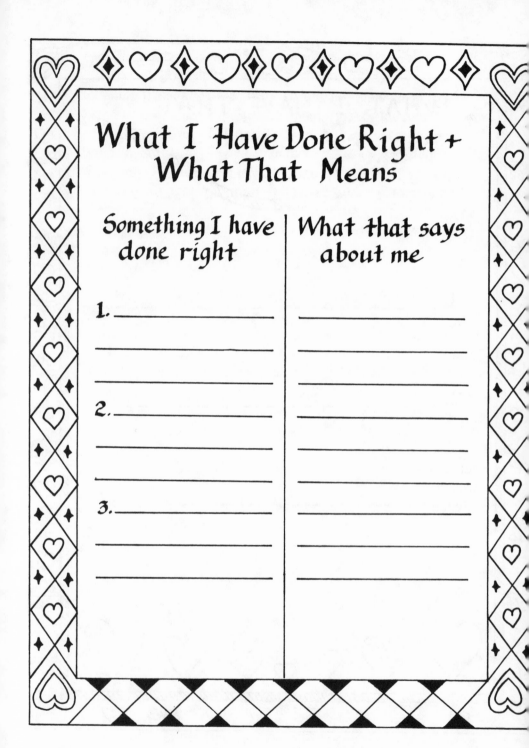

What I Have Done Right +
What That Means

Something I have done right	What that says about me
1. _____	_____
_____	_____
_____	_____
2. _____	_____
_____	_____
_____	_____
3. _____	_____
_____	_____
_____	_____

D: Sure. It could be a new bike. It could be just about anything. I'm sure the kids will help us with this one. I've never met a group of kids yet who couldn't tell me some things they would like.

Y: O.K., children. Who would like to go first?

At the conclusion of this activity, plan to have Do-It return.

Activity #6: What We Have To Do To Get What We Want

Using the list that was developed in the previous activity, help the children divide their wishes into two groups: those that are relatively easy to get and those which seem more difficult to get. With both lists, children should be encouraged to figure out what they have to do to make the wish come true. Here, you may be surprised by the creative brainstorming abilities of the youngsters. Despite their limited cognitive ability, children can be incredibly creative, especially when it comes to figuring out how to get something they want.

Challenge the children. Ask them to imagine that they actually had this "want." How would their lives be different? In what ways would they be happier? Ask them if there would be anything bad about having this wish come true. You may need to point out logical consequences to three year olds. Many of them simply will be unaware of the dangers which might accompany some of their wishes. Still, with sufficient guidance and support, children age four and older can begin to appreciate the consequences of their behavioral choices.

Activity #7: A Happy Book Activity

Have children complete the "What I Have To Do To Get What I Want" page in their *I'm Learning To Be Happy* book which asks them to identify three wants (at least two should be things they can get pretty easily) and the behaviors they will have to use to make these pictures become reality.

What I Have To Do To Get What I Want

Some things I want	What I need to do
1. _____	_____
_____	_____
2. _____	_____
_____	_____
3. _____	_____
_____	_____

Activity #8: The Artist

Have the children paint or draw pictures of things that make them happy. You can then ask the children about their art work and write their answers on the on the painting or drawing.

Activity #9: Building Happiness

At home or in school, have children use blocks to build something that makes them happy. Regardless of whether the children build farms, zoos, or entire cities, their creations represent a part of their personal picture albums.

Activity #10: Scrap Books

Parents and teachers can help children gather together photographs of happy times (birthdays, holidays, playing a favorite game, etc.) and place them in their own special scrap-books. To make this activity even richer, have children dictate their descriptions of the significance of each picture and write their stories under each picture.

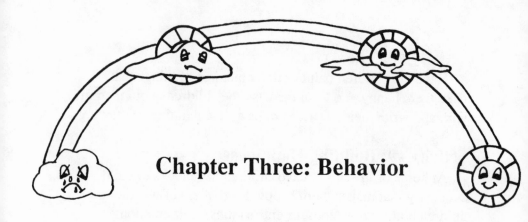

Chapter Three: Behavior

Just as our signals are constantly telling us if we are getting what we want, our behavioral system is working all the time to help us meet our needs. Our behavior is made up of four parts, and all four parts work together contributing to every behavior we ever engage in. These four parts are: acting, thinking, feeling, and physiology. Remember Sarah, the infant whose cries brought her mother? Most of us would identify Sarah's behavior as "crying," calling it by the most obvious of the four components that make up a total behavior. The crying was the acting part of Sarah's behavior. She was also thinking, perhaps that she wanted her mother or that she didn't want to be in her crib. Because of her age, her thoughts may not have been fully formed, but some type of thinking occurs in every total behavior. Feelings were also involved. Sarah may have felt lonely, sad, or even frightened. If she hadn't been picked up promptly, feelings of frustration may have become part of the total behavior. Finally, every behavior involves physiology. In Sarah's case, her behavior included the production of tears, a flushed face, and increased blood pressure, all physiological aspects of her total behavior. While most of us will probably continue to label behavior by its most overt or obvious component ("Tim's yelling." "Mary's depressed." "Becky hit me!"), remember that in every total behavior there is acting, thinking, feeling and physiology.

Most people have been trained over a long period of time that they have no control over their feelings. In one sense, this is true. It's hard to start feeling cheerful when you are feeling depressed just by deciding to feel different. Still, we can significantly affect the way we feel if we remember that feelings are only one component of behavior and all four components work together all the time. We can control what we think and how we act, and if we substantially change our thoughts and actions, our total behavior will be different and so our feelings will change. In essence, therefore, we do have considerable control over our feelings, even though it's indirect control. Put simply, if you want to feel better, do something different. If it helps you get more of what you need, you will feel better.

A difficult lesson for many people to learn is that you choose all of your behaviors, even those which include unhappiness. Once you get a negative signal, you begin behaving in an effort to get what you want. You always could do something else, so your behavior, even though it has become fairly automatic and habitual, really is a choice. As difficult as this may be to accept at first, accepting this fact ultimately empowers and liberates you as you come to realize that starting today you can make more effective choices, get more of what you want, and become a happier person.

Just as it is critical to acknowledge that all of our behavior is chosen, it's critical to remember that all of our behavior is chosen because, at the time, we believe that it represents our best chance to get what we want. No behavior, no matter how ineffective it is or how "stupid" it might appear to someone else, is done without reason.

Even though behavior is chosen, don't interpret that to mean that it's easy to change behavior. Behaviors become habits, and habits are difficult to break. A child who has developed the habit of yelling out in class instead of raising her hand will struggle as she tries to replace the yelling out with new, more acceptable behaviors. The child who chooses an aggressive response to frustration will encounter difficulty as he tries to substitute more appropriate choices for his aggression. To appreciate how habitual behaviors become and how difficult it is to break established patterns of behavior, try this experiment. Fold your arms across your chest. One hand is placed over your opposite arm and your other hand is tucked under its opposite arm. Now quickly fold your arms the opposite way! I'm sure many of you had difficulty changing this simple, value-free behavior. You probably felt awkward putting your hands and arms in the "wrong" position. The purpose of this experiment is to help you experience how difficult it is to change established, habitual behaviors. This doesn't mean you don't try to change behavior, but it does mean that you should not expect immediate, positive results with little effort. Setting realistic, achievable goals will make it easier for you to tolerate the slowness that accompanies most permanent, meaningful behavioral change. It will also make it easier for you to accept the slowness which accompanies meaningful change in the behavior of children.

Ineffective behaviors are those behaviors which do not help you get what you want and frequently only serve to aggravate the situation. Effective behaviors are those which help you get what you want in the long run and which do not interfere with you or the people around you meeting their needs. Between ineffective and effective behaviors are a whole group of behaviors which are best called "band-aid" behaviors. In the long run, these behaviors are ineffective, but they often appear effective because they provide us with short term relief and trick us into believing that they are really helping us get what we need. Name calling, teasing, and scapegoating are typical band-aid behaviors engaged in by millions of children, both at home and in school. These children feel better for the few minutes they are putting down another child. The behavior does address the need for power, but it also frustrates the need for love and belonging and is rarely helpful for very long. Many band-aid behaviors, including the examples just given, also are correctly labeled "irresponsible" because they prevent others from satisfying their basic needs. While every one of us will continue to use ineffective and band-aid behaviors occasionally, with some work we can increase our use of effective behaviors.

At this point, a bit of space should be set aside to discuss a particular cluster of band-aid behaviors used by many people, including some young children: aggressive behaviors. Aggressive behaviors are chosen by people in an attempt to satisfy their needs, frequently the need for power. Somewhat less obvious is the use of aggressive behavior to help satisfy the need for love and belonging. Many children want to be "friends" with the class bully, if for no other reason than it reduces their chances of being a victim. To a lesser extent, aggressive behavior may be chosen to help satisfy the needs for fun and freedom, too. Agressive behaviors are not truly effective because they prevent other people from meeting their needs. Any behavior which interferes with other people's efforts to satisfy their needs is irresponsible and irresponsible behavior can never be considered effective. Our goal in working with young children is to help them develop a large repertoire of effective, responsible behaviors from which to choose. When we help young children learn to behave responsibly, we give them a better chance to live happy lives.

The effectiveness of any behavior depends upon how directly it addresses the unmet need which triggered the signal. If you acknowledge the signal, identify the thing that you want in your life right now, and take effective steps designed to help you get it, you will feel significantly better. If, instead, you merely recognize that you're unhappy and choose a behavior that makes you feel good, but does not directly address the unmet need, you will feel somewhat better, but not as good as you could feel. Let's suppose that Emily, an only child, gets a negative signal. The signal is trying to tell her that she cur-

65

rently needs more love and belonging, but there is no one available to play with and both of her parents are busy right now. Emily's behavioral system comes up with the idea of working on a puzzle. She feels better because she is good at putting puzzles together, and the activity helps to satisfy her needs for power and fun. By changing her total behavior, the feeling component also changed. Still, because Emily's choice did not directly address the unmet need that triggered the signal, she doesn't feel as happy as she could have if she had played with a friend or her parents. To be truly happier, it's critical to understand the message given to us by our signals and to find a behavior which allows us to satisfy the currently unmet need. This issue has particular importance to parents and teachers who redirect children when their behavior is disruptive or inappropriate. To be most effective, determine what need the child was attempting to satisfy with the disruptive behavior, then offer him an opportunity to engage in an appropriate activity that will address the same need. If a child is misbehaving in an effort to achieve power, and we engage him in a group activity which addresses the need for love and belonging, his disruptive behavior may diminish for a time, but he still will be driven by his need for power and may soon become disruptive in the group. If, instead, we can involve him in an activity where he can meet his need for power appropriately, there is far less chance of his being disruptive. In short, redirecting misbehaving children can be an effective disciplinary strategy, but its effectiveness will be enhanced if the child is directed towards an activity which allows him to satisfy the unmet need which triggered the inappropriate behavior.

The objective of the series of activities in this chapter is to help children learn the differences among ineffective, band-aid and effective behaviors, and to increase the number of responsible, effective behaviors available to them to help them meet their needs.

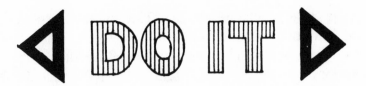

Activity #1: Different Kinds Of Behavior

Use Do-It to introduce the following dilemma to the children. Derek and Jason both want to play at one of the learning centers, but there is only room for one of them. Both receive internal signals, telling them that their needs are not being met. Here are some behavioral options available to these boys:

(1) *Ineffective:* Jason can walk away when Derek threatens to punch him if he doesn't get out of the way. Jason's behavior is ineffective because it does nothing to help him get what he wants.

(2) *Band-Aid*: Derek can threaten to punch Jason if he doesn't get out of his way. Derek's behavior appears effective as Jason moves away, but it is not responsible because it denies Jason the chance to satisfy his needs. Also, aggression is ineffective in the long run because Derek will ultimately lose his friends, thwarting his need for love. *Band-Aid:* Jason can cry when threatened by Derek. While Jason's behavior appears effective in the short run because it results in adult intervention, in the long run it doesn't help Jason meet his need for power or competence.

(3) *Effective:* Derek and Jason can agree to either take turns or both can wait until there is enough room at the learning center for both of them. These choices are effective because they allow both boys to meet their needs and there are no "losers."

Do-It will help the children begin to distinguish among ineffective, band-aid, and effective behaviors by discussing the examples above. Of course, children will have the most difficulty with band-aid behaviors because they give temporary relief and appear to be effective. The concept is especially relief and appear to be effective. The concept is especially difficult for children to master because they live very much in the present tense and have tremendous difficulty appreciating the long-range effectiveness of their behavioral choices. Many adults, too, confuse band-aid and effective behaviors, so don't be particularly alarmed if your children have difficulty with this concept. Do-It can help the children by carefully questioning them about some of the possible negative consequences of using band-aid behaviors.

Another key aspect of this activity is the process of brainstorming. With your help, children will come to realize that there's almost always more than one behavior to choose from, that they never "have to" do this or that, and that more effective behaviors can be chosen if they learn to take a minute to think.

Here is a sample dialogue for this activity.

You: What's up for today, Do-It?

Do-It: Behavior, doing. Remember last time we were talking about some of the things we would like to have?

Y: Sure I remember.

D: Well, today we're going to talk about how we behave in order to get what we want.

Y: I hear lots of people talking about doing what they have to do to get what they want.

D: It's not easy, because some behaviors may help us get what we want but hurt other people. We don't want to do that because everybody has the same basic needs we've been talking about and it's not fair to make it hard for other kids to satisfy their needs.

Y: Would you give us an example, Do-It?

68

D: Sure. Let's imagine two boys, Derek and Jason. Both of them want to play at one of the learning areas in the room, but there's only room right now for one of them. There's lots of things they could do, right?

Y: Yes. I understand.

D: For example, Jason could just walk away if Derek threatens to hit him. Why isn't that a good choice for Jason?

Y: Because if he does that he won't get to play where he wanted to.

D: That's right. Whenever we choose a behavior that doesn't help us meet our needs, we call that behavior ineffective.

Y: Are there other kinds of behavior?

D: Oh, sure. The trickiest is the next kind. We call them "band-aid" behaviors. That means they look like they help, but they really don't. Let me give you an example and see if the kids can figure out what the problem is.

Y: That sounds like fun.

D: O.K. This time, kids, pretend that when Derek tells Jason he's going to hit him, Jason cries and tells a big person. Why is that not the best choice for Jason to make? Can any of you kids figure out why crying doesn't help Jason so much?

At this point, you, Do-It, and the children can discuss how Jason's crying makes it difficult for him to meet his need for power. Children may also concentrate on Jason getting a reputation as a cry baby and losing friends, frustrating his need for love and belonging. The critical issue here is that you help the children realize that Jason's behavior initially appears effective, but actually makes it difficult for him to satisfy his needs in the long run.

Y: So, Do-It, if band-aid behaviors don't really help us, what should we do?

D: The best kind of behaviors are called "effective." When you use effective behaviors, both you and the other person are able to get what you need.

Y: Would you give us an example?

D: I could, but let's see if the kids can figure out something Derek and Jason could do so that both of them are able to meet their needs. Does anyone have any ideas? Remember, both boys want to play at the same place, but there's only room right now for one of them.

Have the children offer Do-It suggestions for effective behaviors to resolve Derek and Jason's dilemma. During the discussion, be certain that Do-It offers some examples of effective behaviors if the children cannot come up with one independently. For example, Derek and Jason can agree to take turns or they could agree to wait until there's room for both of them. After discussing effective behaviors with the children, conclude the dialogue with Do-It.

Y: Well, thanks, Do-It. We'll try to remember everything you told us.

D: Good. The important thing to remember is that effective behaviors are the best, and effective behaviors let everyone satisfy their basic needs. And one more thing: you have to practice effective behaviors. It's not always easy, but you'll be glad you took the time to learn. Good luck, kids. I'll see you again soon.

Below is a list of problems that young children typically encounter at one time or another. In a group, have the children offer various suggestions about how to "solve" the problems. As always, the activities suggested here can be done individually, but this particular series of activities is especially well suited to group work because the children experience the process of brainstorming.

Try not to judge the suggestions as they are made, and discourage the children from passing judgment before the list of suggestions is complete. Encourage creative solutions. It helps the children to focus on the thinking component of total behavior. Also, the best, innovative solutions often grow from impractical, but creative ideas. After the list is completed, the children should try to decide if the solutions are ineffective, band-aid, or effective.

It is probably wise to discuss only one problem during a sitting. You can use the activity for several days in a row or come back to it periodically to review the concepts of ineffective, band-aid, and effective behaviors. The cognitive demands of the activity, however, are such that it would be wise to work in short bursts rather than trying to discuss several situations at one time. Perhaps the ideal situation, once the children have gone through this activity a couple of times, is to use actual problems that come up during the day. That would allow you to take advantage of real "teachable moments," and the problems would be much more interesting and relevant to the children since they would involve either them or their peers.

1. Katherine and Rachelle are on the only two swings in the playground. Meredith comes over and wants to join them. Katherine and Rachelle tell Meredith, "Go away. We're swinging and there's no room for you." Meredith leaves crying.
2. Matthew is playing with blocks, not bothering anyone. Allen keeps knocking over Matthew's buildings and running away. Each time Allen does this, Matthew yells at him.

3. Erika and Karin are best friends and like to play together. Today, as frequently happens, they are arguing about what game to play.
4. Sam is having a wonderful time playing outside. When it is time to come in and listen to a story, Sam cries and complains that he doesn't want to come in, that he never gets to do anything he wants to do "in this dumb school (house)."

Activity #2: A Happy Book Activity

After working through the previous problems, children can choose a particular problem they would like to work on and develop some effective solutions to solve the problem. Depending on the group, children may or may not be helpful to each other. Frequently it is easier to solve someone else's problem than it is to solve your own. This activity presents a wonderful opportunity to assist children in a positive way with some of the ineffective, possibly disruptive behaviors they display. Encourage children to identify problems which they can overcome with relative ease. As the children gain practice in solving problems successfully, their self-esteem will improve. Later, they will be better equipped to tackle more difficult problem behaviors.

"A Problem I Have & Some Solutions" in the *I'm Learning To Be Happy* book can be used to identify a problem and some responsible, effective behaviors a child can use to solve it. (When a child successfully overcomes a problem, it gives you the opportunity to add "overcomes problems" to the child's "Things I Do Well" page, a wonderful way to build self-esteem.)

A Problem I Have:

_____

Some Solutions:

_____

_____

_____

_____

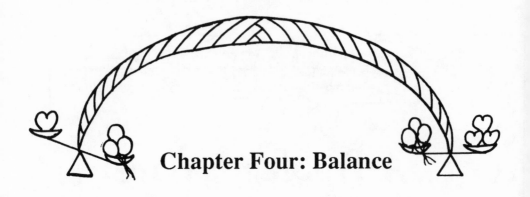

Chapter Four: Balance

If you aren't currently meeting your basic psychological needs (love, power, fun, freedom) in a balanced way, you are not as happy as you could be. Since people meet their needs through other people and activities, one key to happiness is to make sure that you have enough people and activities in your life so that you can meet all of your needs in a balanced way.

I believe the most successful early childhood education programs are those which are designed with this concept of balance in mind. You can take a first step towards increasing the success of your program right now if you will take some time to evaluate the activities you currently use and determine what needs they address. Even if your program is filled with wonderful, satisfying activities, you may discover that it is out of balance. Don't be surprised, for example, if you find your program a bit short on activities which help children satisfy their needs for power or freedom. Once you have done an assessment of your current activities, you can begin to supplement your program with activities that address any deficits you discover.

Parents, too, can utilize the concept of balance in dealing with their children at home. Make sure you give your children not only love, but opportunities to meet their needs for power and freedom. One simple way to help children meet their need for power is to expect them to be as self-sufficient as they can be. Being responsible for simple household chores helps a child become responsible, builds self-esteem, and helps satisfy the need for power. Giving children choices and making them aware that they do make choices helps them meet their need for freedom. Choices can simply be letting your child decide which of the two bedtime stories you have preselected will be read. Remember, the key to happiness is satisfying all of the basic needs in a balanced way on a daily basis.

As difficult as it is for us, as adults, to achieve balance in our lives, it is even more difficult for children. Young children have the same needs that we have, but don't have the same capacity to satisfy their needs, especially for power. Remember, too, that each of us has our own pictures of how we want to satisfy our needs, and the pictures of young children are quite different from the pictures of adults. Watch a typical two year old for awhile. That unequivocal "No!" and "Me do it!" and "No like that one!" that you hear are all clear declarations that even very young children are motivated by the need for power. Even younger children are just as driven to satisfy their needs. You may never witness more motivation and determination than when you observe a five month old struggling for an out-of-reach toy or a nine month old struggling to pull herself up in the crib, or a thirteen month old fall again and again as he learns to take his first steps across the room. All of these struggles are undertaken to establish competence, to gain recognition, to satisfy our in-born need for power.

Think about all the "misbehavior" children engage in at school to meet their need for power. If we were to develop activities which would allow them to satisfy the need for power within teacher sanctioned activities, they would be less driven to misbehave in our classes. I believe that in our early childhood education programs we have done a wonderful job of creating environments where children can meet their needs for love and fun. We have been less successful, however, at creating environments where children can meet their needs for power and freedom. As children grow older, it becomes increasingly difficult for many of them to satisfy their needs in school as they frequently hear such comments as, "You're not here to have fun," or "You're not here to socialize!"

Let's look at two examples of children who are good at meeting some of their needs, but lack balance in their lives.

Kristin, four years old, lives with both her parents in an upper middle class suburb. An only child, Kristin is showered with love, attention, and gifts by her parents and other relatives. She attends a preschool program three days a week and is well liked by the other children in the program. Her teachers find her somewhat "immature," but very compliant and easy to manage. Kristin plays actively and appears to have lots of fun with her classmates. Despite all this, Kristin's life is not in good balance because she doesn't have enough opportunities to meet her need for power. Ever since Kristin was an infant, her parents, both well educated, have done everything to make Kristin "the happiest little girl in the world." In the process, Kristin has never had to struggle for anything, and any time her parents have seen her even slightly frustrated, they have come to her rescue. The result is the "immaturity" seen by Kristin's teachers. Her self-help skills are underdeveloped, and Kristin has had very few opportunities to develop the self-esteem necessary to satisfy her need for power. Because Kristin is so well cared for and her parents are so well intentioned, it's difficult for people to realize that she is a young girl who is less happy than she could be because her life is not in balance. If we were to visualize a circle of Kristin's basic needs, it would look something like this:

Jeffrey is in the third grade. His mother, a single parent, is a very serious woman who has impressed upon Jeffrey the importance of "paying attention and not fooling around in school." Many of the people who live in their neighborhood are unemployed and undereducated. Jeffrey's mother is determined "that my son doesn't become like them. He's going to make something of himself and not be dragged down by any bad influences." Jeffrey is not allowed to accept invitations to other children's homes and his mother keeps visits from other children to a minimum. Jeffrey, who does very well academically, shows signs of being a gifted child. Still, he interacts very little with his classmates and appears sullen and withdrawn much of the time. Since Jeffrey gets good grades in school and his mother lavishly praises him for his achievements, he is meeting his need for power satisfactorily. His relationship with his mother helps him meet his need for love, although he is somewhat deprived in this area because he has such limited access to friends. Jeffrey makes choices every day, but is still quite restricted by his mother, so his need for freedom is not adequately met. Still, the most glaring unmet need for Jeffrey is fun. Despite, or perhaps because of, his mother's good intentions, Jeffrey has been asked to be much more serious and cautious than most third grade students, and he has had very few opportunities to have fun. Jeffrey's Basic Needs Circle might look something like this:

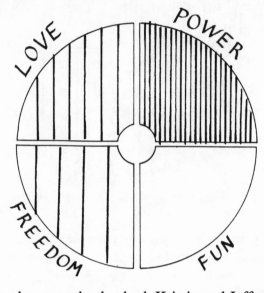

Despite the strengths that both Kristin and Jeffrey have, neither child is as happy as possible because their needs are not satisfied in a balanced way. Remember; to achieve happiness, we must satisfy each of our basic needs in a balanced way on a daily basis.

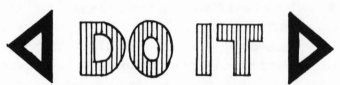

Balancing Your Needs

Activity #1: Basic Needs Circle

This is a fun activity which should offer you a view of how successfully your children are balancing their needs. You may find this activity particularly helpful with those children who don't seem particularly happy, but you haven't been able to figure out just why. Their answers to this activity may help both of you realize what need or needs are not being met.

The object of this activity is to have children complete a Basic Needs Circle. Begin by having Do-It help the children generate a list of important people and activities in their lives. Remember, we satisfy our needs by interacting with others or by engaging in activities either alone or with others. As usual, it may be advantageous to begin this activity as a group, but this is not necessary.

You: Good morning, Do-It.

Do-It: Hi, everybody.

Y: What's that you've got with you?

D: This? (Showing a Basic Needs Circle) This is a Basic Needs Circle.

Y: What's it for?

D: Remember the basic needs we keep talking about?

Y: Sure: love, power, freedom, and fun, right?

D: That's right. Well, this circle has a space to help us figure out how we meet each of these needs. Here's one for love. Here's one for power. Here's fun. And here's freedom.

Y: But there's nothing on it.

D: I know. That's why I came. I was hoping the kids would help me fill out a Basic Needs Circle. Would you kids be interested in helping me?

If this activity is done in a group setting, it is wise to make a "group" Basic Needs Circle. It will draw on the strengths of many children. You will end up with a balanced circle, and the kids will all get to experience the process of completing the Basic Needs Circle. The activity, of course, can also be done individually.

D: O.K. Let's start with people. Can you think of someone who really loves you, even if they sometimes get angry with you?

Do-It should take a few names from children and you can list them in the "Love" quadrant of the Basic Needs Circle.

D: Let's do this section called "Power." Can you think of someone who tells you that you do things well? Some-one who thinks you've got some good ideas?

Do-It will choose the names of several people for you to list in the "Power" quadrant.

D: Great job! Now let's do the section that says "Fun." Who is a person you like to play with? Someone who makes you laugh? Who helps you learn new things?

Again, Do-It will choose a few names for you to include in the "Fun" quadrant. If the activity is being done in a group, have Do-It call on a variety of children so that everyone feels involved and important. Continue to make lists of all the other things Do-It asks for in the appropriate quadrants of the Basic Needs Circle.

D: O.K., kids. The last section of the circle says "Free-dom." Who are some people who let you make choices, who let you make some decisions about what to do?

Y: Thanks, Do-It. We have a nice circle filled with people who help us satisfy our needs.

D: But we're not finished yet! We meet our needs through people and activities. We still need to list the things we do to help us meet our needs. Come on, kids. Let's start with love again. Who can think of something that you do that makes you feel like you're part of a club or group?

D: O.K. Now "Power." Someone tell me something you do well.

D: Great. Let's do Fun. Let's think of some things that are really fun to do, something you really enjoy doing.

D: And now Freedom. What is something that you do where you really get to make choices and decisions?

D: Now we've got it! This is a beautiful Basic Needs Circle that includes lots of the people and activities you have to help you meet your needs. I'm glad we did this. After I leave, maybe each of you can make your own Basic Needs Circle, just for you!

Y: Thanks, Do-It. I think we'll want to do that someday soon.

D: I'd like to see them when they're finished. Remember to have fun when you're doing it! See you soon!

Activity #2: A Happy Book Activity

After children have completed answering Do-It's questions about each important person and activity, they are ready to complete the Basic Needs Circle contained in their *I'm Learning To Be Happy* books. Each person and activity should be considered separately to determine what needs are met. If a person helps a child meet all of her needs, list them in each quadrant of the Basic Needs Circle. On the other hand, if a

81

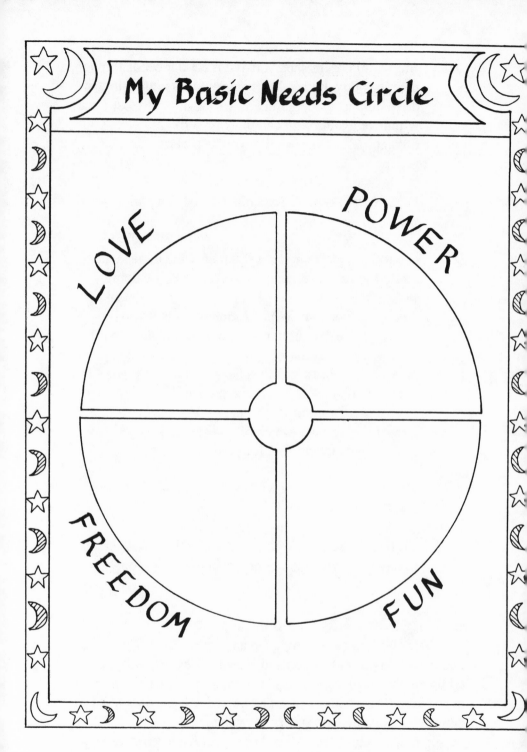

My Basic Needs Circle

LOVE

POWER

FREEDOM

FUN

person helps a child meet only one or two needs, list that person only in the appropriate quadrant(s). When each child has finished this activity, you will have completed a Basic Needs Circle for each child which identifies the people and activities important to each of your children in their attempts to meet their needs.

The Basic Needs Circle is useful for two reasons. First, as the adult, you can quickly identify children whose needs are not balanced when you see one or two quadrants which are empty or close to empty. Secondly, the Basic Needs Circle is important for you and the children because it identifies for each of you, in specific terms, how the children go about satisfying their needs. This will come in handy when children get negative signals and get stuck trying to figure out what to do to feel happier. It's not always easy to figure out what to do when you're feeling down. By completing the Basic Needs Circle, however, you and the children can refer to it and identify people and activities that have been sources of happiness in the past.

The real value of this activity will be determined by how honestly the children answer your questions. Some children, both because they want to please and because they may have difficulty understanding some of the concepts involved, may give answers that aren't particularly helpful. For example, even if Matthew doesn't usually play with Randy, on the one day the two boys happen to play well together you may be given distorted information. Matthew may make it seem as if Randy helps him satisfy all of his needs when, in fact, the truth is very different. Also, children may enjoy this activity so much that they answer "Yes" to every question. You will have to use skill and powers of discrimination to help children create a truly valid Basic Needs Circle. Instead of relying solely on the information the child provides during the activity, be certain to use what you have observed and what you know of the child to help you.

To help get you started, here's an example of a Basic Needs Circle, thanks to my children:

Maintenance

Activity #3: A Happy Book Activity

Whether children's Basic Needs Circles revealed balance or not, the objective now is to build on whatever strengths they currently have. There will be time later for them to take specific steps to create better balance in their lives; the first step is to help them maintain those things they currently do which help them satisfy their needs. Too often, we look for solutions without giving enough attention to whatever successes we already have. Emphasizing our deficits does little to help our self-esteem and failure to recognize and maintain our strengths can result in losing those skills we do have. This activity is designed to help children recognize what they already have and to help them practice behaviors which have been successful for them in the past.

Children should do this activity individually, with adult assistance, using the Basic Needs Circles they have completed. You can use Do-It to help you with this activity if you want.

KEEPING UP the GOOD WORK

1. In order to continue _____

   I will _____

2. In order to continue _____

   I will_____

3. In order to continue _____

   I will_____

The "Keeping Up The Good Work" page in *I'm Learning To Be Happy* asks children to identify three things from their Basic Needs Circle which they would like to maintain.

It is important for children to realize that good things exist in their lives because of behaviors they choose. If they want to continue experiencing the happiness they currently enjoy, help them identify specific behaviors they can use to continue meeting their needs.

Children can be remarkably vague in their description of behavior. Encourage them to be specific when completing this activity. For example, "I will be his friend" is not nearly as helpful as "I will make sure to invite him to play a game with me." Also, encourage the children to identify issues and behaviors which they can do relatively easily and regularly. Having successful experiences will help build their self-esteem.

Activity #4: Make a Mobile

Have children make a mobile by crossing two straws and hanging yarn from each of the ends. On each of four 3"x5" index cards write one of the basic needs (love, power, fun, freedom). Show the children as you help them attatch their cards to the yarn, that their mobile isn't balanced unless all of the cards (needs) are hanging on the mobile. In the center of the mobile, hang a card with the child's name on it. The mobile represents the child, balanced by all four needs.

Activity #5: Expand the Mobile

After completing the previous activity, ask the children to write on index cards the names of people and activities which help them satisfy each of their basic needs (one person or activity per index card). The cards should be labeled according to the need satisfied by that particular person or activity. Children can then hang these index cards on their mobile under the corresponding need and actually see if their lives are in or out of balance.

CHOCOLATE ♡ VANILLA ♡ STRAWBERRY

Chapter Five: Options

As adults we recognize the importance of having many options to choose from as a means of achieving happiness. When I went to college, my parents encouraged me to take enough education courses to become certified as an English teacher "just to keep your options open." Options, however, are just as important for children. My son Greg loves music, and at the age of three he announced that he wanted to play the cello. When he turned four, my wife and I signed him up for lessons, but he was told that he was too small to play a cello and would have to begin with a violin. Because Greg was able to switch pictures quickly (he only chose misery for a short time and decided it wasn't particularly satisfying), he has been able to pursue his love for music and finds that playing the violin satisfies his needs for love and belonging, power, and fun. If he hadn't been so flexible, Greg would have missed an opportunity to create happiness for himself. Quite simply, options give us more opportunities to satisfy our needs and experience happiness.

It is critically important for all of us, even young children, to develop options, alternative behaviors designed to help us meet our needs. If Laura only achieves a sense of power when she is painting and her scheduled painting class has just been cancelled, she will be in trouble. Her need for power will be as strong, but she will no longer have any behaviors she can use to meet this need. Similarly, if Tim experiences fun only when he is swimming and he lives in New England where he has limited swimming opportunities, he will still be driven to satisfy the need for fun but will have no behaviors available to help him for much of the year.

Options can provide us with insurance if things don't turn out the way we want. As adults, we know only too well that things frequently don't turn out exactly as we had hoped. Our task is to take things as they are and still find a way to satisfy our needs. The more flexible we are, the more options we have of how to satisfy our needs, the more likely we are to be happy, even when things don't go as we planned.

Does this mean that flexible, creative people are never un-happy? Of course not! But flexible, creative people, people who have developed more options, are less likely to wallow in their misery and are more likely to decide to take some steps to be as happy as they can be in any given situation.

In Chapter Two we discussed pictures. When we talk about options, it might be helpful to think of developing as many pictures as possible for each of your basic needs. In this way, if something goes wrong and one of your pictures is no longer available, you still have other pictures available to choose from so you can continue to satisfy your needs and lead a happy life. Again, this doesn't mean you don't feel the loss you have suffered. Still, you choose not to be paralyzed by that loss, but instead choose to be as happy as you can be.

Children need to develop options, too. If Melanie is only going to have her need for love and belonging met by being with someone in the immediate family, she's going to be miserable at school. While it's likely that her family members will always remain prominent pictures for her, she will have to develop acceptable alternatives if she's going to be happy at school. If Greg has a picture of fun which would be satisfied by playing the board game Sorry and we can't find the game, it would be helpful if he could substitute Parchesi as a picture to satisfy his need for fun. If Kristy has a picture in her head of dancing to satisfy her need for power, and ultimately she decides she simply is not talented enough to pursue dancing as a career, she will still have a need for power and will be a happier adult if she has developed alternative pictures, perhaps teaching dance to young children.

We will be helping children tremendously if we teach them at the earliest possible age to develop acceptable options. Children should be encouraged regularly to think of as many ways as possible to satisfy their needs. Just as importantly, they should actually engage in a variety of behaviors so they can experience alternative ways to meet their needs for love, power, fun, and freedom. The more options they have available, the more resilient they are, the happier they will be. Children benefit from being taught options because it gives them a greater sense of control over their own lives. They are more willing to accept the responsibility of their own happiness when they have been given the skills to create it effectively, responsibly, and regularly.

It is probably easier to teach options to young children than to adults. Adults tend to have their pictures very much in focus and know exactly what they want. They are less likely to settle for alternative pictures, and many adults actually choose to be miserable, at least for awhile, rather than choose another picture. Children are generally more flexible. If Greg wants Frankie to come over to play and Frankie isn't home, Billy is usually an acceptable substitute. The beauty of teaching options to young children is that it is easy and gives them the message from a very early age that there are a variety of ways to satisfy their basic needs. If one pathway is blocked, another pathway can be found. As was discussed in Chapter Three, behaviors become habits. Exercising your options is one habit you'll be glad you developed.

Remember, every one of us, young and old, must satisfy all of our needs every day in order to be happy. The more options we create for ourselves, the more happiness we will experience.

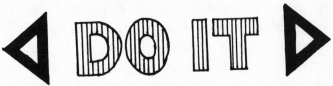

Creating A Balanced Basic Needs Circle

Activity #1: A Happy Book Activity

In many ways, the chapter on Balance is the central chapter in this book since balancing our needs is critical to achieving happiness. This activity is designed to help those children who don't have sufficient balance develop some alternatives so that they can begin to balance their needs more effectively.

Look at the "Adding Balance To My Basic Needs Circle" page in the *I'm Learning To Be Happy* book. You will see that each quadrant of the Basic Needs Circle is divided into two sections: one for those people and activities which the child already has, and one for those the child could add to create more options and better balance. With your help, children should complete the "Have" section using their completed Basic Needs Circle from the earlier page. You may use Do-It to work with the children on this activity.

Activity #2: Things We Would Like To Add

In this activity, Do-It assists the children as they complete the "Add" section of their Basic Needs Circles they have been working on in their *I'm Learning To Be Happy* books. The "Add" section can be approached in several ways. Children can work on this activity individually with help from you and Do-It. It is also possible for children to share their Basic Needs Circles with each other so that they can get new ideas about people and activities they may want to add to their particular Basic Needs Circles. Or some type of combination approach

Adding Balance To My Basic Needs Circle

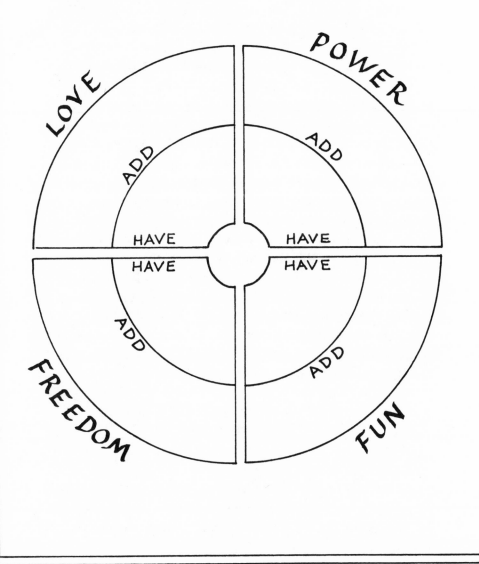

could be used to complete the activity. Regardless of which approach you choose, all the children should end up with specific people and activities which they can add to their lives in order to satisfy their needs effectively in a more balanced way.

Do-It should discuss some of the options outlined below with the children. This will help them see that there are various possibilities available to include in the "Add" section of their Basic Needs Circles. A sample dialogue follows.

Where To Look To Create More Love & Belonging In Your Life

- Is there another child in my class or neighborhood I would like to get to know better?
- What are some of the things I like to do? Are there other children who would like to do this with me?
- Can I take part in any activities where I can meet other children? (arts and crafts, music, play group, sports, etc.)

Where To Look To Create More Power & Recognition In Your Life

- I get power and recognition for the things I do well. What are some of the things I do well now? (read, ride a bike, know my colors, etc.)
- What are some of the things I could learn to do to get more power and recognition? (play a new game, get dressed all by myself, learn to spell more words, etc.)

Where To Look To Create More Fun & Pleasure In Your Life

- I have lots of fun when I learn new things. What new thing could I learn?
- When was the last time I heard a joke? bought an ice cream cone? made popcorn & watched a movie with my family? went to the park? went on a picnic? went someplace special with my family?

Where To Look To Create More Freedom In Your Life

- People are free when they make decisions. What are some of the decisions I have made today? (what to wear, what activity to do in school, what to eat for lunch, etc.)
- People get freedom by making things. What is something I can make today that would help me feel free? (a model airplane, a drawing, a pinwheel, etc.)
- I feel more free when I move. When am I going to dance so I can feel more free?
- Even though I'm still young, I need free time, too. Starting today, I'm going to have some time every day when I can do whatever I want to do as long as it doesn't hurt anybody and doesn't break any rules.

Sample dialogue with Do-It:

Do-It: Good morning, kids. I hear you have all been working on Basic Needs Circles.

You: That's right, Do-It, we have. The children have already completed the "Have" sections of their circles and now we're going to work on the "Add" sections. Would you like to help?

D: I'd be delighted to. O.K., kids, please take out your Basic Needs Circles. See where it says "Love"? It looks like you've got some people and activities there already. Now let's think about other people you might want to be friends with, or games you could play, or places you could visit to meet even more people. Who can suggest something?

Use some of the suggestions made by the children and include a couple in the "Add" section of the "Love" quadrant. Continue to list suggestions in the other quadrants as Do-It asks for them.

93

D: Great. Let's add to the "Power" section. Can anyone think of something they could learn to do well to get more recognition? Or is there some activity you could do where you would get to be the boss, even if it's just for a little while? Being in charge makes people feel like they have some power.

D: How about "Fun"? Learning is fun. What are some new things you could learn about? What are some other fun things you would like to add to your circles?

D: And let's not forget about "Freedom". What are some ways you could add more freedom, more choices to your life?

D: Wow! Look at that Basic Needs Circle now! Not only do you have lots of things already, there are a whole lot of things you can add to your lives to make them even happier.

Y: Thanks for helping, Do-It.

D: It was my pleasure. Thanks, kids. I'll see you again real soon.

Start Adding Happiness Now

Activity #3: Do-It Helps To Make a Plan

The first two activities in this chapter were designed primarily to help children think about how to balance their needs more effectively. Our ultimate goal, however, is to help children actively create their own happiness, not simply think about creating it. The objective of Activity #3 is to translate the thinking done in the previous activities into a specific plan of action. Do-It leads a discussion about some of the things children included in the "Add" sections of their Basic Needs

94

Circles. Then the children choose one issue to work on collectively, brainstorming with Do-It about what they need to do to get what they want. At the end of the activity, Do-It will have taken the children through the process of developing a specific plan to add more happiness to their lives. Here's a sample dialogue to show you how the discussion might go.

You: Good morning, Do-It. You seem especially happy this morning.

D: I am because I have something special to tell the kids. Are you going to ask me what it is?

Y: Sure, Do-It. What do you have planned for today?

D: Well, you know how we've been working on our Basic Needs Circles?

Y: Of course I do.

D: Well, today I want to talk about how we can actually have some of the things we put in the "Add" sections of our Basic Needs Circles!

Y: That sounds exciting.

D: It is. Let's get going. Can I have a volunteer?

The remaining dialogue is for illustration purposes only, as each child will, in fact, have different things in the "Add" section of the Basic Needs Circles. For this illustration, I have chosen something many children would like to have—another friend.

Y: I think Valerie has something she would like to add to her Basic Needs Circle.

D: O.K., Valerie. Let's see what we can do. What do you have in the "Add" section that you would really like to work on so you can put it in the "Have" section?

Valerie: Well, Do-It, I have lots of things.

D: Good, Valerie. That shows that you've been thinking. Before we pick one, remember that you'll have to do some work. You can't have things just by wanting them. It has to be something you're willing to work for.

V: Well, Do-It, I have lots of friends, but I'd like to have even more friends because sometimes my friends are sick or have other plans and I have no one to play with.

D: O.K. if you want someone else for a friend, someone else to play with, what do you need to do?

V: I can wait for them to invite me over their house to play.

D: Sure, but suppose they don't invite you, even if you wait for a long time?

V: Then I'd be sad.

D: Waiting for someone else may not be the best way to make sure you'll be happy. Someone may invite you over because you are very nice, but they might not invite you. So what can you do to make another friend?

V: I could invite someone to my house to play!

D: Exactly! Have you thought of who you would want to invite?

V: I'm not sure yet.

D: Then we need to do some planning. Let's begin with who you would like to play with. Who would you most like to add to your list of friends?

V: I think I would pick Robin.

D: O.K. When would you like to have Robin over to play?

V: Today!

D: But you haven't asked your Mom, right?

V: Oh, yeah. Well, tomorrow would be alright.

D: When will you ask your mother?

V: Today. After school.

D: Suppose she says tomorrow is a busy day and Robin can't come over then?

V: Then I could ask her if we could make it another day. And, after I ask my mother, I'll make plans with Robin.

D: Great, Valerie. That's how you can move something or someone from the "Add" section to the "Have" section of your Basic Needs Circles.

Y: Thanks, Do-It. I think all the children will want to make plans, just like Valerie did.

D: Great! That's what being in control of your own happiness is all about. Just remember, kids, that making plans takes time and work. Make sure you plan carefully so you can really get more of what you want. That's why it's a good idea to have a grown-up help you plan. Well, good luck and happy planning! I'll see you all soon.

Activity #4: A Happy Book Activity

Children are to choose one of the people or activities they have listed in the "Add" section of their Basic Needs Circles, then decide exactly what they will do to move that person or activity from the "Add" section to the "Have" section of their Basic Needs Circle. Of course, children will need your help to plan specific, effective behaviors, but it is important for them to learn that if they want to be happier, they have to do something different. By completing the "Do It" page in the *I'm Learning To Be Happy* book, children will develop a specific plan to add more balance to their lives. Again, you are urged to help children choose wisely. Their choices should be attainable so they will have a satisfying experience that enhances the balance in their lives and helps them learn that they are capable of creating their own happiness.

DO IT

So I can have:

_____

I need to:

_____

_____

_____

Chapter Six: Relationships

Since we frequently meet our needs through interactions with other people, the quality of our personal relationships is an important consideration in our effort to live happy lives. In reality, we need other people in our lives to help us meet our needs, but frequently we find ourselves in conflict with others, especially those we care about most deeply, such as parents, teachers, or classmates.

Often the conflict originates from the different pictures we have of how our needs should be satisfied. Suppose Becky asks Aaron if he wants to do something fun and he agrees. At that moment, each of them has a perfectly developed picture of what "fun" with the other will be. Becky might envision sitting down and playing a favorite board game. Aaron's picture of fun might involve riding bicycles and searching for buried treasure. Ultimately, the success of the relationship depends upon the ability of the people involved to work things out so that both are able to satisfy their needs with the other. If they are unable to do this, either the relationship will end or at least one person will be unhappy.

How do we choose to work things out with those we love when conflict arises? Unfortunately, many of us, young and old, choose behaviors with a very strong feeling component, such as whining, crying, or complaining. We choose these behaviors because we believe that they will get us what we want, and often they seem to be effective, at least in the short run. Young children frequently try behaviors with a strong feeling component. Since tantrums usually aren't effective for long, many children learn quite early in life how to strike a mournful, pitiful pose, often accompanied by a painful series of sighs, in order to get what they want. Misery is a powerfully controlling behavior and many youngsters learn to use it to get what they want. It is pretty easy to say "no" to a screaming, kicking, angry child. It is much more difficult to say "no" to someone who looks so forlorn that you're afraid your refusal might just be the straw that breaks the camel's back. Children whose manipulative, emotional behavior is effective in getting them what they want often grow into adults who use behaviors with powerful feeling components. A friend of mine recently told me about a woman he knows who "suffers from depression. It's so bad she hasn't been able to work for a year." When I asked him if she were able to get out and enjoy herself at all, he told me, "Oh, sure. Last week we went to Fenway Park to see the Red Sox and she seemed O.K. to me. But people tell me she's got this depression and she can't work. It's too bad." People who are "too depressed to work" but quite capable of enjoying an evening out at the ball park have become masters at using misery behaviors in order to get what they want. Until they develop other effective, satisfying behaviors, they will continue to ooze misery.

Even though many people use behaviors with a strong feeling component to get what they want, this strategy is not productive if your goal is to have a good relationship. A healthy relationship is one in which both parties are able to satisfy their needs responsibly. Once someone tries to control you with their feelings, you will receive a strong negative

101

signal because on some level you will know that you are being manipulated, which immediately prevents you from satisfying your need for freedom. Manipulation can come in positive forms (flattery) or negative forms (threats), but in either case, manipulative behavior can destroy a relationship. If you can't meet your needs in the relationship, it becomes unhealthy for you.

Manipulative, controlling behaviors start to emerge very early in life. Young children often learn that a little extra misery can result in a second dessert or can change a parental "no" into a reluctant "yes." How many times have you heard one child say to another something like, "If you don't let me go first, I'll never be your friend again"? Each of my children, at one time or another, has come up to me and said, "You're the best Dad in the whole world," and then immediately asked for something. Every time that has happened, the negative internal signal I received was jolting, because I felt so manipulated. All of us can learn to eliminate some of our controlling behaviors, and as we do, our interpersonal relationships will improve.

In order to help children improve their relationships, there are specific behaviors you can teach them and others you, as adults, can use.

(1) Teach them to tell others what they want in a nice way. If you want someone else to help you meet your needs, he has to know just how you want your needs met. Youngsters can learn how to state their wants in appropriate, unselfish terms. They will have a much better chance of getting what they want if they can communicate what they want.

Like adults, children often believe that other people can read their minds and know what it is that they want. This leads to a lot of needless misery. One objective of the activities in this book is to help children learn how to say what they really want, to improve their communication skills. For those of you who are afraid we will be encouraging the creation of a generation of selfish "wanters," remember we are stressing responsibility in our dealings with children. We are not fostering selfishness, but the development of communication skills which will allow children to meet their needs more effectively in a responsible way. We are willing to help children achieve reasonable, responsible wants, and responsible wants are not selfish, are not manipulative, and do not interfere with anyone else's attempts to satisfy their wants and needs.

(2) Compromise and negotiate. These skills are probably the most critical to maintaining any relationship over a long period of time. Since all long-term relationships will eventually involve conflict, the issue is not how to eliminate conflict, but how to handle conflict effectively. Like it or not, negotiation and compromise are all we can use to resolve conflict responsibly. Anything else results in winners and losers and is not conducive to a healthy relationship.

Negotiation and compromise are skills which lead to both people in a conflict getting some of what they want and all of what they need. The alternative is for the more powerful person to get what he or she wants and the less powerful person becoming a loser. (Ironically, even the "winners" are frustrated because the process of winning can make it difficult to satisfy the need for love and belonging.) Clearly, negotiation and compromise are preferable.

Children are unlikely to understand the terms "negotiation" and "compromise," but that's not particularly important. I have found that my children are able to understand it when I say to them, "You'll have to find a way to work it out so that you're both happy." I then step into the background and let them practice the arts of negotiation and compromise. Of course, since they are so young, sometimes their efforts are less than satisfactory. Still, the only way I can get my picture in the future (being the father of adult children who are accomplished negotiators and compromisers and effective communicators) is to let them practice these skills in a safe environment and only intervene if one child is clearly manipulating the other unmercifully. Just this morning Melanie and Greg were arguing, not an unusual occurrence. Melanie came to me whining, looking for me to join forces with her so she could get what she wanted. After she had told me about her conflict with Greg, I asked, "What are you going to do now?" She just smiled and said, "I guess we'll have to work it out." It was a moment I'll treasure forever. Just as importantly, they did work it out, successfully and fairly.

(3) Say "Yes" as much as possible. You will be amazed at how many problems disappear! This is especially true when you are working with young children. When you say "yes," you are, by definition, a need-satisfying person and become a picture in the other person's album. On the other hand, when you say "no," you are telling someone that they can't have what they want. It's preferable, therefore, to say "yes" even if it has to be followed by a set of conditions. For example, saying "Yes, you can play with Billy once you have cleaned up your room" is preferable to saying, "Absolutely not. Your room is a mess!"

Of course, there are times when, as adults, we need to say "no." Sometimes children want to do things that are against the rules, or things that are dangerous. In such cases, it's both appropriate and responsible for the adult in charge to say "no." Children accept a "no" more readily from someone who usually lets them have what they want. But remember, please, if you do say "no," mean it. Don't weaken and change your mind.

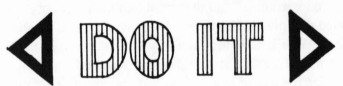

Learn To Say What You Want

Activity #1: Saying What You Want

In this activity, Do-It helps the children learn to communicate their wants in responsible ways and to plan effective behaviors to get what they want. The discussion should center on the following: (1) who the child needs to help him achieve what he wants; (2) what he needs to say; and (3) when he plans to say it. An important part of this activity is for children to learn how to communicate what they want in responsible, acceptable ways. The following dialogue illustrates this process.

You: Hi, Do-It.

Do-It: Hi everybody. I hope you have been working on making plans since I saw you last.

Y: Oh, yes, Do-It, we have. What have you got planned for today?

D: I wanted to do some more work on plans if someone wants to help me. Any volunteers?

Y: I think Corey wants to volunteer.

D: Great. O.K., Corey. We're going to discuss something you want, who you need to tell, what you're going to say, and when you're going to say it. O.K.?

Corey: O.K., Do-It. I want my father to take me to a basketball game.

D: That's a good one to work on. First of all, does your father know that you want him to take you to a basketball game?

C: Well, he knows I like basketball, and he knows I had fun when we went to a game last year.

D: Sure, but have you told him recently that you'd like to go?

C: I guess not. I'll tell him tonight.

D: Not so fast, Corey. You have to figure out the best way to talk to your father.

C: The best way? Don't I just tell him to take me to the game?

D: You could. I'm not sure. Does your Dad work?

C: He's a carpenter.

D: Carpenters work pretty hard. Is he tired when he comes home from work?

C: You bet. He's exhausted and sometimes he's grumpy until after dinner.

D: Would it be smart to ask him before dinner?

C: I get it. No, it wouldn't.

D: Corey, it's important for you to give your Dad some quiet time when he gets home. Let him know you understand that he has needs, too. He'll probably appreciate that.

C: So when should I ask him?

D: Well, I don't know. It's really up to you.

C: He's usually in a pretty good mood after dinner. He usually sits around talking to my Mom and me. I could ask him then.

D: Sounds good. What exactly will you say?

C: That I want him to take me to a basketball game.

D: That might sound kind of selfish.

C: I don't mean it to be selfish. I had fun last time we went and I like doing stuff with my Dad and sometimes he's busy so I don't get a chance to do so much with him.

D: That sounds different. Now it sounds like you want to go to the game so you can spend time with a person you love.

C: Well, that's what I want.

D: Then it's important to say that. That's what I mean when I say planning takes time and is a lot of hard work. You have to let your Dad know that you're not a selfish kid, but a kid who wants to spend time with him.

C: I see what you mean.

D: When are you going to do it?

C: Well, tonight would be a good night, so I'll try to talk to him tonight.

D: Are you going to *try* to talk to him or are you going to talk to him?

C: I'm going to talk to him.

D: O.K., Corey. Good luck. Choose your words carefully, let your father know what you really mean, and I bet things will work out well.

C: Thanks, Do-It.

Y: Thanks, Do-It.

D: My pleasure. You know, I think all the kids would like to do what Corey just did.

Y: Well, guess what? We're all going to make plans, just like Corey did. Thanks for getting us started, Do-It. See you again soon.

Activity #2: A Happy Book Activity

Help children complete the "What I Want" page in their *I'm Learning To Be Happy* book. Be certain that the children pick wants which are responsible, appropriate, and achievable. Don't be afraid of making things too simple. Your goal is not to make sure children get everything they ever want. Your goal is to teach a process so children will have an effective model of how to communicate what they want to others in a responsible, effective way.

We Can Work It Out

Activity #3: We Can Work It Out!

Use Do-It to introduce the "we can work it out" concepts of negotiation and compromise. It is probably best to discuss only one problem a day and do this activity for several days in a row. The best problems to use are those which have taken place in your class or in your home simply because "real life" problems are always superior to artificial ones. Sometimes, however, it's easier to begin with a less threatening, more artificial problem, so I have provided you with a few problems below. A dialogue with Do-It is included for the first problem as an illustration.

(1) The problem: Johnny and Nicolas are fighting over the last tractor to use in the sandbox.

You: What's up for today, Do-It?

Do-It: I'm going to tell you about two children who have a problem. I want to see if you kids can figure out a way for them to work it out so that both of them get what

108

What I Want

1. Something I really want.

_____

2. Someone who can help me get this.

_____

3. What I need to say to them so they'll know what I want.

_____

4. When I plan to tell them what I want. _____

they need.

Y: Sounds like a good challenge. What's the problem?

D: Johnny and Nicolas are fighting over the last tractor in
        the sandbox. Both boys want it. What can they do so
        that they both get what they need, so there are no
        "losers"?

Y: Melanie, do you have a suggestion?

Melanie: Johnny could just let Nicolas use the tractor. Johnny
        probably gets whatever he wants anyway.

D: That's one possibility. Are there any problems with that
        one? Greg?

Greg: Yeah. Johnny doesn't get what he wants so it's not fair.

D: Good point, Greg. So what can we do? Kristy?

Kristy: The boys could agree to take turns so that both get to
        use it some of the time.

D: Excellent! That's a perfect solution. That way both
        boys get what they need. They both win and nobody
        loses.

Y: Is that what you mean when you tell us that we have to
        learn to work it out?

D: That's right. Working it out means that everybody wins.
        If we want to get along with other people, we have to
        learn to work things out. Otherwise, we'll always have
        trouble with other people and that's not the way to be
        happy.

Y: Well, Do-It, we all want to thank you for everything you've taught us.

D: I've enjoyed myself. The important thing to remember is that we have to practice everything we've been talking about. But it's worth the work because in the end you'll learn how to make your life much happier.

Y: Thanks again, Do-It, and good-bye.

M: Good-bye, kids. Remember, I'll never be very far away. Whenever you want me, just give me the word and I'll be glad to help you find ways to lead happier lives. So long for now. Be happy!

(2) The problem: Kristy and Jen have split a can of soda. One girl is going to have hers in a glass and the other will get the can. Both want the can.

(3) The problem: You allow the class to choose, from an appropriate list, what movie they can watch at a special event party. One half wants to watch "E.T." and the other half wants to watch "Star Wars."

Activity #4: A Happy Book Activity

Children should not complete the "We Can Work It Out" page in their *I'm Learning To Be Happy* books until they have had some time to think about different ways people can work things out. Once you feel they are ready to complete the individual exercise successfully, you can help them (1) identify a problem they were having with someone else, and (2) what they did to work it out so that both people got what they needed. Make sure you help children choose situations where some negotiation and compromise actually took place. Don't let them choose as examples situations where they used power to win or where they gave up everything to the other person just to avoid conflict. An important aspect of this activity is

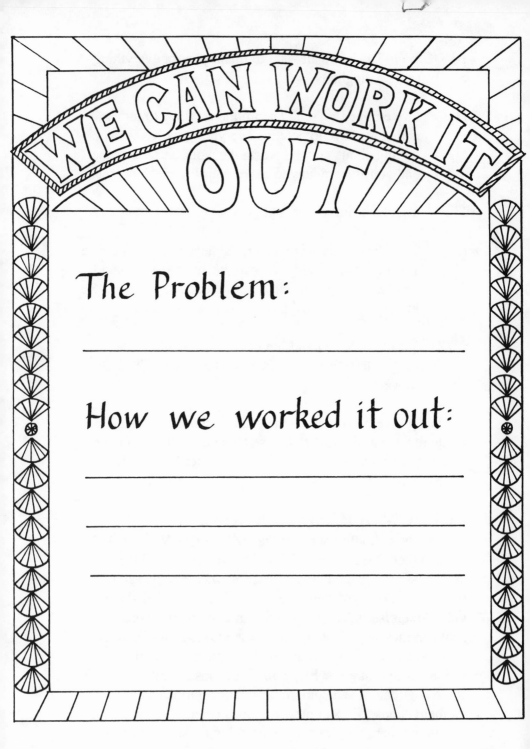

WE CAN WORK IT OUT

The Problem:

_____

How we worked it out:

_____

_____

_____

that children realize they actually have worked things out successfully. As with many of the other activities they have done, a successful experience helps to build their self-esteem.

Make Someone's Day

Activity #5: Positive Bombardment!

Here is a delightful activity whose objective is to have children practice saying positive things about other people. It is wonderful for group time at schools or at dinner with families. Have every person in the group say one positive thing about each other person. (At the dinner table, everyone should participate in this activity, regardless of their age!) This will give children practice in complimenting other people and help them build positive relationships. Also, hearing good things about themselves helps to satisfy their needs for love and power. This activity almost always is a wonderful success. It can make meal time a more positive experience in any home. I strongly urge everyone to make this activity a regular part of your routine, not a one or two time event.

Activity #6: A Happy Book Activity

Have individual children complete the "It's Nice To Be Nice" page in their *I'm Learning To Be Happy* books where they are asked to indicate something positive they have said to three other people during the past week. It is best to do this activity a week or two after the previous activity so that children will have no difficulty thinking of the nice things they have been saying recently.

IT'S NICE TO BE NICE

1. I told _____ that

   _____

2. I told _____ that

   _____

3. I told _____ that

   _____

Chapter Seven: Creativity

Our imaginations are constantly generating new behaviors which we could select in our efforts to solve problems and meet our needs more effectively. Even those of us who claim not to be particularly creative have a creative system which is always "on." If we are willing to try, most of us can gain access to our creative selves fairly easily. The advantage of having easy access to our creativity is that it will offer us more options to choose from and more opportunities to meet our needs responsibly. The more able we are to find effective, responsible behaviors, the less likely we are to act on the "crazy," irresponsible behaviors our creative systems offer us as well.

Young children can be taught to be more creative in two ways. First, I encourage you to teach the process of brainstorming. If you have conducted the activities suggested in this book, then your children have already been exposed to this process. I recommend brainstorming as a regular problem-solving technique to use with children. It teaches them that alternatives are

115

always available to choose from. It helps children appreciate that problems frequently have multiple solutions, and consequently, it helps prevent children from falling into the "right or wrong" answer trap which often applies in school but is of little value in the world at large. Brainstorming is a fun activity which encourages children to focus upon the thinking component of behavior, expanding their cognitive abilities. Finally, brainstorming fosters creativity.

The second avenue to creativity, a "quiet time" activity, is something that can be integrated into an educational program or may be done with children at home. Just as adults can gain access to their creativity by regularly engaging in a non-competitive, relaxing, pleasurable, solitary activity, children can start to establish a similar behavioral pattern in their lives. In our zeal to provide "meaningful" and "structured" experiences for our children, many of us have overbooked our children's days. While structure is a wonderful thing, children whose lives are overly structured have little capacity to utilize unstructured time responsibly and effectively. Such children tend to behave less creatively because their overly structured lives dictate to them how they should behave at all times.

All children should have 30-60 minutes each day of what I call "quiet time." This time should not to be spent watching TV, nor should it be spent socializing. Children should spend this time entertaining themselves, reaching into their creative systems. Building with blocks, playing a musical instrument, looking at books, coloring, drawing, painting, working with clay, or "just thinking" are all appropriate behaviors during quiet time. Whatever activity is chosen (it can be different activities on different days) should have the following characteristics:

(1) It should be non-competitive.
(2) It should not require a great deal of effort and the child should be able to do it reasonably well.
(3) It should be one which the child can do alone.
(4) Most importantly, the child should be completely self-accepting during this time. If the child is at all self-critical

when doing this activity, it will lose much of its therapeutic and creative value.

Most of us would agree that adults would also profit from a daily "quiet time". We live in an overstressed society and have paid a high price, including denying ourselves access to the creative solutions our behavioral system has to offer. Even those of you who will never incorporate such a routine into your daily lives because "I just don't have the time," probably are acutely aware of its intrinsic value. If that's the case, help your children avoid the same difficulty. Teach them from the earliest possible age to slow down each day, to take time for themselves, to have a time every day when they are completely self-accepting, and to listen to their creative selves. Behaviors that become habits are difficult to change. Why not turn that sometimes frustrating fact into an advantage by helping children develop a behavioral habit which will strengthen them? (Those of you who are interested in learning more about how to tap into your own creative system are encouraged to read *Positive Addiction* (1976) by Dr. William Glasser where these ideas are presented in detail.)

Don't expect that children will become noticeably more creative after a daily "quiet time" routine has been established at home or in school. The fact is that young children tend to be more creative than adults anyway. They have fewer barriers and inhibitions to overcome. What you offer children will not necessarily enhance their creativity immediately, but it will provide them with a model for behavior which will become increasingly valuable to them as they get older, when creativity diminishes in many people. The immediate benefit to children will be that they will be engaging in a self-accepting activity which they enjoy every day. That, by itself, will help build strength and lead to greater happiness.

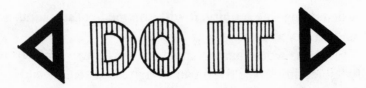

Activity #1: Quiet Time

Set aside a half-hour, or whatever time you can manage, for children to do individual "quiet time" activities. Discuss with the children the characteristics of an appropriate quiet-time activity, then give the children some time to make suggestions. Each child should pick an activity for the quiet time and do it. Daydreaming, thinking, doodling, and "nothing" are all acceptable activities.

Summary

As Part II draws to a close, it's important to summarize what we can do to help young children.

We can teach them about the basic needs which will motivate them for the rest of their lives.

We can teach them about the specific pictures they develop to satisfy these basic needs.

We can teach them to recognize both their positive and negative signals.

We can teach them that they choose how to act, even if they don't have direct control over how they feel.

We can teach them that all behaviors have consequences, that they create most of their pleasure and their pain.

We can teach them how to develop options so that they have a better chance of getting what they need.

We can teach them how to plan, to organize a series of behaviors, so they can get more of what they want.

We can teach them to be responsible, to behave in ways that allow other children to satisfy their needs.

We can teach them how to have better access to their creative selves.

In short, we can TEACH THEM TO BE HAPPY !

ACTIVITIES FOR
A BALANCED CLASSROOM

In *Teach Them To Be Happy* I have given suggestions about how to work with children at school and at home to help them achieve happiness by learning to satisfy their basic needs regularly and in a balanced way. Teachers would benefit enormously if they had a pool of activities to choose from which would ensure that all children have an opportunity to satisfy their needs for love, power, fun, and freedom every day.

I invite you to participate in my project, the creation of a book filled with age-appropriate, satisfying Activities for a Balanced Classroom. Educators will be able to select from model activities which their colleagues have found to be successful in such a way as to achieve even greater balance in their programs.

If you are interested in contributing one (or several) of your favorite, successful activities, I would be delighted to hear from you. Simply supply the information listed below with as much detail as possible. Feel free to share this information with your colleagues.

Contributors are encouraged to send activities as soon as possible. Publication will commence once a sufficient number of quality contributions have been received, and contributions will be considered in the order in which they are received. Contributors whose activities are selected for publication will be acknowledged as contributors and will be given a complimentary copy of the the first edition of the book in which their contribution appears. Accepted contributions may be edited and their final form may differ somewhat from what is provided.

Submission Form for
Activities for a Balanced Classroom

All contributions should be typed, double spaced, and include all of the information requested below.

Address all correspondence to: Robert A. Sullo, PO Box 1336, Sandwich, MA 02563.

(1) Name of Activity:

(2) Indicate the need or needs addressed by this activity:
    LOVE   POWER   FUN   FREEDOM

(3) Level for which this activity is most appropriate (please
    indicate only one):   pre-school
                               grades K-1
                               grades 2-3

(4) Content Area:
    language arts   math   health & safety
    social studies   art   drama
    science   music   other (please specify)

(5) Objective of the activity: (Exactly what are the children
    expected to do either during or at the conclusion of this ac-
    tivity?)

(6) Materials required:

(7) Procedure: (Be as specific as possible, explaining exactly
    how to do this activity.)

(8) Any additional comments that you think might be helpful:
    (i.e., Is the activity easy or difficult to organize? Is the
    activity one which can be done at any time, or should the
    group be together for a while before it is attempted? etc.)

(9) Contributor's name as you wish it to appear:

(10) Your personal address and telephone number: (This information is for my use only, in case I need to contact you to get information, seek clarification, etc. Only your city or town and state will be published.)

In accordance with the Copyright Revision Act of 1976, you must submit the following statement, signed, before your submission can be considered for publication:

"In consideration of Robert A. Sullo taking action in reviewing and editing my submission, the author(s) undersigned hereby transfer, assign, or otherwise convey all copyright ownership to Robert A. Sullo in the event such work is published by him."

Contributor's Signature and Date:

SUGGESTIONS FOR FURTHER READING

Books about Control Theory and Reality Therapy

Glasser, William, *Reality Therapy*. New York: Harper and Row, 1969. This pioneer book about Reality Therapy provides a fascinating account of the use of the process of Reality Therapy with most difficult cases.

Glasser, William, *Positive Addiction*. New York: Harper and Row, 1976. A complete description of how to add positively addicting, strength-building activities to your life.

Glasser, William, *Control Theory*. New York: Harper and Row, 1984. A complete description of the theory upon which the process of Reality Therapy is built. A must for anyone who wants to understand Control Theory in detail.

Glasser, William, *Control Theory in the Classroom*. New York: Harper and Row, 1986. Primarily geared towards issues in secondary schools, this book details how to implement Control Theory principles in school systems. Especially interesting and important are the sections on cooperative, or team, learning.

Good, E. Perry, *In Pursuit of Happiness*. Chapel Hill, NC: New View Publications, 1987. Details the essential elements of Control Theory and provides the reader with useful activities designed to help people take more effective control of their lives.

Wubbolding, Robert E., *Using Reality Therapy*. New York: Harper and Row, 1988. A valuable resource for any serious practitioner of Reality Therapy, this book outlines how the process of Reality Therapy can be effectively applied in a variety of settings.

Books about Child Development

Brazelton, T. Berry. *Toddlers and Parents*. New York: Delacourte Press, 1974. Written by a pediatrician from Children's Hospital in Boston to describe the individual characteristics of very young children and the stresses that parents typically experience rearing children.

Chess, Stella et al. *Your Child is a Person: A Psychological Approach To Parenthood Without Guilt*. New York: Penguin, 1977. Authors are three professors of child psychiatry who describe development from birth through first grade. Normal variations in both social development and learning styles are discussed. Authors try to reduce parent guilt about children's behavior by identifying what is within normal limits. Includes a chapter about preschool children with special needs and another on identifying emotional-behavioral problems which require intervention.

Elkind, David. *The Hurried Child*. Reading, MA: Addison-Wesley, 1981. An important work for all parents and educators. The author discusses the consequences of hurrying children and urges a return to a less stressful method of raising our children.

Greenspan, Stanley and Nancy Thorndike Greenspan. *First Feelings: Milestones in the Emotional Development of Your Baby and Child*. New York: Viking, 1985. Describes six stages of emotional development which occur throughout the first four years of life. Discusses how to recognize the child's needs in each stage. Provides information about the interaction between parent personality and the needs of the infant/child.

Pulaski, Mary Ann Spencer. *Your Baby's Mind and How It Grows: Piaget's Theory for Parents*. New York: Harper and Row, 1978. Written by a child psychologist to describe the stages of intellectual development and day-to-day activities.

Even though it makes Piaget more easy to comprehend, this still represents complex reading.

Segal, Marilyn and Don Adcock. *Your Child At Play.* New York: Newmarket Press, 1985. This is a series of four separate books written for parents on the value of play and how to facilitate and participate in play with children ages: Birth to One Year; One to Two Years; Two to Three Years; Three to Four Years.

Stallibrass, Allison. *The Self-Respecting Child.* New York: Pelican Books, 1977. Describes the importance of play in the first few years of life. Describes circumstances with children ages two through five that afford appropriate chances to develop learning skills, social interaction, and self-esteem.

White, Burton. *Educating the Infant and Toddler.* Lexington, MA: Lexington Books, 1988. Child psychologist writes about stages of development with an emphasis on how early experiences lay the foundation for all social and intellectual development. Contains a review of books, videos, and additional resources available to parents.

Books To Use With Children

Aliki. *Feelings.* New York: Greenwillow, 1984. Excellent book to read with children.

Fariotta, P. and N. *Be What You Want To Be: The Complete Dress-Up Pretend Crafts Book.* New York: Workman Publishing, 1977. A very practical book which gives information on how to make props for pretend play.

Freed, Alvyn M. *TA For Tots.* Rolling Hills Estates, CA: Jalmar Press, 1973. Excellent pictures and text to help children understand emotions and how they can better meet their own needs.

Hagstrom, Julie. *Let's Pretend*. New York: A & W Visual Library, 1982. A practical book with ideas for specific pretend play themes for young children.